(US edition)

'Anyone who has ever dreamed of picking up and moving to a totally new world should enjoy this book ... a loving, wistful story'
Phyllis Meras, *Providence Journal*

'Much more than a good travelogue. [Emma Tennant] has captured the personalities of the islanders as well as their idiosyncratic customs – things only a person living in a culture for some time can know'
Julie Hatfield, *The Boston Globe*

'Exercise caution when reading this book – it's likely to induce a serious longing to hop on the next flight to Greece'
Booklist

'A delightful memoir ... [Emma Tennant] eloquently renders the stark beauty of the landscape, the seductive, treacherous sea, the delicious cuisine and her family's friendships with local residents whose customs the newcomers came to understand and respect. This account of an alternative lifestyle ... will appeal to travelers, expatriates and their admirers'
Publishers Weekly

D0280478

Corfu Banquet

a memoir with seasonal recipes

EMMA TENNANT

with Maria Mazis

summersdale

Copyright © Emma Tennant, 2004

Summersdale Publishers Ltd
46 West Street
Chichester
West Sussex
PO19 1RP
United Kingdom

www.summersdale.com

ISBN: 1 84024 381 3

The right of Emma Tennant to be identified as the author of this work has been asserted in accordance with sections 77 and 78 of the Copyright, Designs and Patents Act 1988.

No part of this book may be reproduced by any means, nor transmitted, nor translated into a machine language, without the written permission of the publisher.

Printed and bound in Great Britain

Cover photograph © The Travel Library

Portraits of Corfu copyright © Christopher Glenconner

London Borough of Hackney	
Askews	HBS
949.55	£7.99
	04/400

Contents

Chapter One

Spring

We used to call them the Kali Spera Club, the old women who popped out of nowhere in the olive groves on the way down to the house. '*Kali spe-era*' drawn out so the evening greeting comes like a sigh of relief after a baking hot day working the land and piling the donkey with bundles of sticks and greens before heading home. Then '*Herete*' as we stumbled past: a 'Hello' so much more friendly than anything you're likely to get in England. 'But only if you hail them first,' a friend explains, who has spent a lifetime travelling in Greece. 'If you don't, they'll ignore you and you'll find you're invisible.'

We've done the journey to our house, Rovinia, so many times before that people here know us and we call out to each other at the same time. There's Yorgos, coming out from his house on the road that leads down to Yefira Bay.

He looks ready for the talk and long, ruminative silences that accompany his ouzo when he's sitting out at our back door, just across the woodland overlooking the sea. There's Constantina his wife, who dresses up as evening falls and wanders along the beach under the cliff where my father and mother built their house nearly forty years ago. She looks, as ever, like an operatic heroine and wears the distracted air of one who spends hours at a time sorting the thin filaments of the fishing nets on Rovinia Bay's stretch of shingle and sand. She, too, will join Yorgos, and Maria and Thodoros, the couple who live part of the year at Rovinia and look after the house, out on the back porch; and here the almost-wild cats will gather hungrily on recognising the fisherman and his wife. The last scrapings of the bucket were tossed out at ten or eleven this morning, when Yorgos and his friend Yannis returned in their small boat: a *barbounia* (red mullet) too small to cook, perhaps the head of a monkfish – Yannis' prize catch – and a handful of tiny, whitebait-like creatures for them to gobble greedily. Now, like us, the cats will be back again, seeking the treats Rovinia can offer. It's that kind of place.

The just-completed road is one of the much-anticipated surprises in our journey out to Corfu (Kerkyra in Greek) this year. It's the middle of March, and midwinter as far as the locals are concerned, with only a wisp or two of smoke rising from land about to be cleared. Swimming pools, dozens more of these each time we come, lie either side of the road that leads down from Liapades village to the sea. They're empty, and look like huge teardrops fallen from a sky that is already a gorgeous Greek blue. Won't it be a bit of a rush, getting them cleaned and filled by May, when the influx of tourists begins? But Tasso, at the wheel of the taxi which has met us at the vast new Corfu airport, shakes his head and swerves wildly as the car turns up what will be 'our' turning to a new road we have never seen in its entirety. '*Oxi*,' he laughs. 'No.' '*Tipota akoma*,' (nothing yet) and we are reminded that Greek Easter, the great watershed in the country's calendar, is over six weeks away. There will be *tipota* for a long time to come, before the sudden need for a rush opens the supermarket with its baskets of chocolate eggs and shelves of vegetables that look as if they've been left undisturbed all winter long. Even the tiny bar, no more than a couple of tables and four chairs, has the air of being open by mistake. It is to this bar that Tim goes for his evening pint – and has gone, or to another like it up in the village, for the just over a quarter of a century we've been together. But if you run out of a necessity up in Liapades, this is the only place you can buy it. And neither Tim nor the ever-changing stream of visitors from Yorkshire who take rooms in the house opposite the bar mind rootling in the fridge for their own beer when they come in for a drink.

We're in Tasso's taxi because our own car, a two-door Ford bought second-hand many years back, turned over on a muddy road recently. (Thodoros, who drives and looks after the car while we're in England, and his grandson little Spiro escaped, thankfully, unhurt.) The whole rigmarole of buying a car in Corfu will have to be gone through all over again, once we've settled in, and it's my mother, domiciled in Greece, who must visit the Government offices, produce endless documentation, and unravel the arcane laws surrounding the should-be simple act of acquiring a car. 'It's going to be hell,' she says, as we turn sharply left off the road to Yefira, with its hotels and closed tavernas and carpets of wild flowers, pink and purple and blue rising to greet newcomers on both sides. 'It'll take weeks, and we'll just have to be patient,' she warns. But the restrictions do sound ludicrous, now the euro has become currency; the Olympics are a couple of years away; and the EU has splashed out so much on improving the amenities of the country.

'Yes, only one new car permitted to be bought in a lifetime,' Tim concurs. 'And if you import a second-hand car there is a huge tax, introduced to prevent foreigners from buying cars abroad, bringing them in and reselling them for a hefty profit.' It doesn't seem surprising that no one at home can understand these difficulties. So my mother has had only one new car, bought by my father in the 1970s, and she has bought second-hand ever since.

'We certainly do need a car,' she remarks quietly, as Tasso charges skyward and then turns down by a sign where a wag has scratched out the lettering, so we have ROVINIA OUS, and has spun the post for good measure, guiding visitors over a steep ditch into an olive grove.

Each time you arrive at Rovinia it's different – even if it's also magically the same. The new road has made redundant the painful walk down cliff, along slithery path and over archaic cobbles that we used to have to do. No more suitcases strapped to our bodies while rain and thunder showed us just who is boss on a Greek island where the local plane from Athens frequently has to turn back, its load of returning travellers praying to St Spiridon, patron saint of Corfu, to save them. No more stumbling to the top of the steps that lead down to our house and terrace and wishing – though this lasts no more than two minutes – that we had gone to a comfortable hotel on the other side of the island instead. (Here, on an occasion where we were driven to the just-opened Cricketer's Hotel at Yefira by a storm worthy of Zeus' thunderbolt, it was to find beds as cold and wet as the path we'd turned back from. Early Easter then too, and the students offered a special rate by hotels in Corfu in order to warm up tourist beds in advance of '*to saison*' hadn't appeared yet.)

Thodoros' cousin Spiro is responsible for this new road, funded by Rovinia and the village both, and last seen in a perilous half-surfaced state, with the autumn downpours just about to begin. 'It looks great,' we encourage Tasso, as his face, normally the picture of Greek good humour, droops badly.

'Sort of ribbed cement,' I add, trying to help.

'I think this bit was done only last week,' my mother agrees nervously.

It's turning into evening, on this day that's not like others after all. The first sighting of the sea far below is as strange and wonderful as we've been expecting – blue that turns to Homer's wine-dark in one long swathe of colour as it sweeps under the cliff where our house can just be glimpsed, the red-tiled roof like a child's drawing. Along with the sheer drop on the left-hand side of Spiro's adventurous road, it quite takes the breath away. 'The poles have been placed there,' my mother notes with approval, as we look out at what appear to be giant knitting needles positioned alongside the drop. 'That'll make it all much better, I'm sure.'

To take our minds off the shock of seeing familiar landmarks totally altered by the positioning of this brave new road, we discuss the times we've returned to Rovinia before, to be greeted by Maria's stories of those who rented our house in the heat of high summer. 'The *Barone* is a *kalos anthropos*' (a good man) Maria had declared the year before, and it had taken a little time to realise that the person she referred to had actually been the Duke of Kent. Why he liked to be known as a *barone* we never knew. 'His wife was unhappy that the boat had no canopy,' Maria had gone on. We all knew it could reach 40 °C in August, and a guilty silence followed this particular recollection. Our little blue and yellow boat, made ready each summer by Thodoros for trips down the west coast of the island, was still without a canvas roofing. Thodoros would go out fishing for hours on end in the hottest weather, as we all reminded ourselves – but then he wasn't the Duchess of Kent. This time, we vow, we won't forget to have an awning made up in the town. 'The *Barone* had only four toes,' Maria had gone on recklessly. But this assertion even her most credulous listeners refused to entertain.

By the time we've stared out at the sea and swapped tales from Maria's repertoire – how John Barrymore rented Rovinia and danced with her in the kitchen, how the rich American woman started on the gin at 9 a.m. and was joined by her husband an hour later on whisky, every day of their visit – we're in the last stretch of Thodoros' cousin's road. The *kali speras* rise to meet us as we climb from Tasso's taxi and make our way down the tall, mosaic-pebble steps to the terrace. It's so early in the year that the vine over the path leading to the back door has only tendrils of a piercing bright green. Evening falls, as it seems literally to do in Greece; one minute the sky is the colour of the blue door where Maria stands, arms outstretched in greeting, and the next it's so dark you can't see. Lights go on, shining on the rough walkways as we go down. A new type of cat, pale ginger and white, a Corfiot bird-hunter as we are to discover, comes out to meet us, followed by a grey-striped companion and then more. The moon is suddenly visible, high in the sky. We are here.

Rovinia today is much as it was when it was first built in the mid 1960s, a white, blue-shuttered house, with three bedrooms upstairs and a long white room downstairs with a vaulted ceiling. The floor tiles aren't shiny but a pale matt rose, and all those years ago when they went down looked as though they were about to crumble to dust, but never have. There's a guest wing – which isn't a wing at all, for to get to it involves walking down a narrow path bordered at this time of year with pink and white cistus, two kinds of broom and gorse, and wild flowers that succeed each other in waves: speedwell, mallow, asphodel and orchid. The 'wing' can be frightening for those who don't relish the Corfu thunder and lightning when it comes, or the crash of waves, for the sea is directly below. A porcupine's nose of sharp, scaly rock juts out beyond the wing and descends steeply into an ultramarine ocean, for it's deep here, out beyond the beach. Tim and I often choose to sleep in the wing, but at Easter it can feel as if the weather has come too close for comfort and it takes ages for the beds – without the necessary influx of students – to dry out. Behind the house are two buildings: a studio where my father painted happily through the last eighteen years of his life, and the house where Maria and Thodoros live, which looks out onto my mother's sunken garden, all white with syringa, canna lilies, white roses and lemon blossom. The place has become so overgrown now, almost four decades since the side of the hill was hacked out to make foundations for the house, that it's hard even to see the different houses. Walls are covered by jasmine or roses, and vines are trained on trellises and will yield muscat and strawberry grapes when summer comes. Only at this time of year, when the figs are putting out tiny emerald leaves and the irises are not yet swallowed by long grass, can the original shape of the house be seen.

Today is our first day at Rovinia for nine months, and we've chosen to sleep in the spare bedroom in the main house rather than risk the wing. Because of this, when we wake we see from out of the window the astonishing change that has taken place on the beach, and we find we're running down there to check that something magical and surprising really has happened at Rovinia, as it so often seems to do. Last year the torrent came down the riverbed in one great *swoosh!* bringing with it a mass of old tins and masonry and a brown stain which spread out into the sea for days. What can have happened now, when only last June we were expressing disbelief and horror at the swathe cut in the lovely beach by the sheer volume of water that had descended on it, cutting a new – and not very beautiful – landscape from earth and sand and shingle. How can the sea have come up to meet the new estuary formed by last year's disaster and made it all anew?

'It's incredible!' we say as we race down the steps, not even looking out to see if today's wonderfully unseasonal bright sun has brought an asp or an adder, eager to warm itself, on to the steps. 'It's created the perfect beach!'

Maria and my mother are there before us and we stand in silence on sand as soft and golden as a film set. Where once there had been a great deal more pebbles than sand – and that gritty, good for children's mud pies type of sand, but uncomfortable for swimmer and sunbather – there is now a holiday brochure vision, a real sandy beach stretching politely down to turquoise water. 'It couldn't have been brought here for tourists now there's a road down to Rovinia, could it?' we joke.

It's impossible to know how many winter tempests changed the course of our beach. But the sight of little Spiro, grandson of Maria and Thodoros, as he wanders in quiet bliss on the sand makes the question seem unimportant. 'Let's go up to the taverna on the hill near Skripero,' I suggest when Spiro begins to ask for his father Nicos, who with his wife Dimitroula runs the Paradise Taverna a half hour's drive away.

'We haven't a car,' Tim points out.

Yet, as if the new beach and the glorious feeling of a new spring coming to Corfu had filled everyone with life's possibilities, Maria points out that her son Nicos is coming down here anyway. 'He has a lovely car and will take us all up to Paradise.'

In this latest visit to Rovinia, what stands out most is the way the island is changing, thanks to tourism, and how some of the changes, contrary to received opinion, actually improve the way life is lived here, for residents and visitors alike. The airport, once a series of dismal sheds with a sense of hopelessness induced by a frequently broken luggage carousel and toilets which can only be described as old-style Greek, is now huge and gleaming. Leather seats make the obligatory passing of hours before the flight is called pleasant and far from the days of standing ankle-deep in discarded Styrofoam and pistachio shells. In villages so remote they're literally off the map, shops selling organic honey and halva have sprouted. And in Sula, our local supermarket, everything can be found, from pegs and nails to Irish whiskey.

Of course, there are changes to our private paradise, too. The publication of *A House in Corfu* has caused readers to come down the new road to the house and explore Rovinia. Once the early spring of our arrival begins to turn to summer, more visitors will appear on the beach, and in our last visit I found Thodoros gravely showing a young woman around the house. 'She said she must see the rooms,' he explained. And my mother's struggle in the government offices to obtain permission to buy a car was lessened by the sudden intervention of the policeman on duty there, who recognised the address and announced proudly that his English wife Kate was reading the book. (None of this prevented another week's wait, as the island had inexplicably run out of number plates, making the car uncollectable.) So the olive grove and the lovely bay have entered the consciousness of many people. But the path down to the beach has always been open to fishermen and visitors alike.

On the west coast of Corfu, it's easy to forget the rest of the world altogether. So when a writer who is putting a cookbook together rings and asks if she can come over, we feel we've been cut off for so long that it would be good to meet a stranger. The day didn't go well. As our road is hard to find, Tim went off to the Yefira road to guide Wendy – not her real name – and, at my insistence, took my mobile phone with him. Tim is a mobilophobe. When he was standing in the road, the phone rang and a persistent Londoner, not Wendy at all, kept demanding to speak to me. In his desire to get rid of her, Tim turned off the mobile and then couldn't turn it on again. An hour later, Wendy, who had indeed been lost, appeared, and by the time we all sat down to lunch my mother wore a very old-fashioned look.

The first intimations of summer are gloriously here at last, and we sit out more often on the terrace. At lunch we enjoy Maria's latest irresistible dish, *yemistes*, stuffed tomatoes and peppers which contain no meat, just a subtle amalgam of rice, thyme and herbs, which with *rigani* (the Greek oregano, stronger and sharper than the Italian version), grow wild around us. As the days lengthen, we take to evenings when to have a stiff drink laden with the mint that now grows happily here is to salute the sea and the mountain, known for its shape as the monkey's head, as the sun goes down behind it. We go down more and more often to our new perfect beach, to test the water, which is suddenly warm, despite the *Maestro* wind which blows from the north and turns the sea the strongest blue of all. After swimming, we go up and sit in the little front terrace of the Nikterida, our local Liapades taverna, and look out at the vans and the old women with their donkeys as they go up the street, and the new generation of girls on Lambrettas pop-popping off to meet friends in the town. And we say to each other, as we so often have before, that after lunch we'll walk all the way back to Rovinia. But it's too tempting, now there's a new road and a new car, to drive all the way home.

Chapter Two

Scotland into Greece

When my father died at Rovinia in October 1983 he had lived in Corfu since 1965 – probably the happiest years of his life. The views he painted there, of cliffside and Homeric sea, of flocks of sheep in wave-washed coves and steep-stepped village streets, hang in the house today and are admired by visitors drawn upward from beach to terrace by the pebbly path with its border of yellow sternbergia and cyclamens (these in the month of his death, the autumnal month that is the most beautiful of them all). His studio stands empty now, where tiled roofs were marked out with care and precision on his canvases, and a profusion of the spring flowers he loved to paint – the grape hyacinth with its spiky crown, a celebrity chef's haircut in bright mauvey-blue; the marigolds and delicate daisies, three times the size of anything you find at home – crowd the pictures just as they do at the end of the grove each spring. For all the festive aura of the meadows though, the bright skies and fringes of woodland found on expeditions off the beaten track on the Plain of Ropa, just above and beyond our house, it is the plainest scenes that hold one's attention and which remain in the memory once home again. The headland, stark and bare, that sticks out into a darkening sea. Or the sand-coloured hills of Mathraki, the island a few hours' sail away in the big caique: here there are ancient flints and arrowheads in shallow soil and some of the simplicity and mystery come across in the pallor of the oils, faded as the knowledge of those distant times. It's when thinking of these, and of a landscape so austere that nothing grows except a straggle of samphire along the cliff tops, that I am reminded of the country where my father grew up – and then I with him, before being separated by a war that took both my parents away for almost a year, across Europe as it closed behind them. I think of the valleys and hills of Scotland, the Lowland burns and isolated lochs where islands stand out like scars against the steely rippling water. I think – or I thought then, when the telephone rang one October night in London and I heard the news of his death – that it was perhaps the childhood landscape of Scotland that my father had transmuted to Greece and painted all along.

I'm standing in the old kitchen of our house and Bella, who comes in from the village to help Mrs McKay the cook, is visible just outside the door. She's busy in the scullery, which can't have been changed – or even given a coat of new paint – since the days midway through Victoria's reign when Glen, this preposterous imitation castle, symbol of my great-grandfather's financial success, was built. Bella is small, though I don't find her so: I am by far the smallest member of the kitchen staff, as I self-importantly like to think myself at three years old, and my head barely reaches the top of the kitchen's great wooden table. I know what Bella is doing, though, for she has reached for me and lifted me high above the wide stone sink where spinach, most of it tangled with the thick brown Peeblesshire mud of the kitchen garden, is floating in water so cold that Bella's hands have turned to slabs of ice. I scream each time I'm given the treat of being lifted to look down at the spinach: the cold is unbearable and in any case I've spotted Jimmy, gamekeeper here before the War came and he had to join the Home Guard, as he comes in with an animal dangling from one arm and a rifle slung across the other. I would rather be with Jimmy than Bella. Jimmy holds the keys to the kennels down the road where the dogs roam and bark, and I am very occasionally allowed in at feeding time when the porridge and meal are mixed. I am more interested in what the dogs eat – Labradors and border collies, trained for picking pheasants and grouse from a snarl of heather roots and boggy hillside – than in the food Mrs McKay prepares for the dining room upstairs. Except, of course, when flour goes down on the clean, ridged surface of the kitchen table and a jar of currants is brought down from a high shelf by Mrs McKay standing on a rickety chair. I can hear my nurse May, to whose care I have been confided in the absence of my parents, as she comes along the tiled corridor and opens the window that gives onto the tall kitchen with its skylight and a range that swallows coal from a great metal cone and goes out each night, needing to be relit when it's still dark morning. I know May will say we'd better go easy on the currants. There's a war on, and scones with currants just won't be possible soon. There'll be plenty where my mother and father have gone, Mrs McKay will remark. Out there, in Turkey. In Istanbul. But Bella, who has taken the rabbit Jimmy shot and hung it in the freezing larder three steps up from the scullery, lifts the spinach in huge handfuls from the sink and holds it dripping in the air. It looks like the weed at the bottom of the pond where the oars of the rowing-boat get snagged and there's no more fishing until it's all been disentangled. Mrs McKay tells Bella to fetch the rabbit back, after all. I can hear she's in a bad temper, and it's because May has said we'll be in to lunch today – that's my two elder half-brothers and their mother and all. It's not fine enough for a picnic up at the loch, so we'll have the rabbit – and the spinach along with it – though I'll refuse to eat, as so often, and there won't be anyone to report to, with my mother gone and a stranger there instead of her at the dining room table.

Chapter Three

Apricots & Gold

My father had been sent to Turkey to manage the United Kingdom Commercial Corporation on behalf of a department of the Treasury. This was a form of economic warfare, which sought to reduce German influence in Turkey, a neutral country. He and my mother left in June 1940 and were away until the spring of the following year. In their absence, and to ensure their safety from bombing in London, my father's first wife and my two half-brothers were installed in the house in Scotland. We met chiefly at mealtimes; and I remember a dish of peas, tiny and sweet from the kitchen garden, and the younger of my two half-brothers helping himself to the whole dish – until May, indignant at his selfish behaviour, bustled round the table and restored this treasure of early summer to its rightful proportions on each plate. I don't think the boys' mother noticed much of these battles as they took place. She was my stepmother, I suppose (except the old story books in the library, with their wonderful illustrations by Walter Crane, always gave the stepmother as one who had come into the family after the death of the hero or heroine's mother and not as an earlier wife). She was affectionate, slightly scatty in manner; and when the very pale peaches came into season, she would leave shreds of their skin neatly piled together under her fruit fork. She never came up to the greenhouse when I begged to go there, and May had to leave her knitting and her endless cups of tea in the day nursery to escort me up the garden and into the long glass buildings where the smell of tomatoes was succeeded by a waft of nectarine or peach. I almost expected my father, who was overindulgent in the matter of greenhouse visiting, to be there, standing beside the trees espaliered against the white walls. He would bend down to lift me up to a ripe apricot and I would reach for the gold, scented fruit with its slightly freckled complexion and sagging skin. But of course he wasn't there; and May would be warned off by Mr Robson, the gardener. Although, as I was to discover later, there was no way that my parents could have returned in that year through Europe from Turkey, everyone, Mr Robson included, went on as if they were about to reappear any minute. Fruit and vegetables were kept back or made into extra large quantities of jam. But when the season for game opened, grouse and pheasant and partridge could no longer be bagged on the hills and moors: the War prevented that.

Agnes was the name of the cook who took over the antiquated kitchen of the Big House, as the laird's house in a Scottish village – or usually just outside it – is invariably known. She was Czech, and what she must have made of Doug and Jimmy, who came in at any hour with a rabbit or hare, or of the boy who sometimes brought a trout, caught in the loch up at the end of the valley, was anyone's guess. These weren't people who talked very much – though I would be allowed to join in the dancing and singing at New Year Hogmanay celebrations 'downstairs' and they would tell jokes then, and dart quick glances at me to see if I understood their (usually) good-natured jibes about their employers. Neither Doug nor Jimmy, who had spent most of their lives with the dogs down at the kennels on the back road or out on the hill, beating heather or undergrowth to release birds for the guns (the shooting had been let to Americans over past years), could have had much to say to Agnes. The boy who went fishing didn't come from the village, and he said nothing at all when he handed over the brown trout or the occasional salmon poached from the Tweed. Sometimes he simply left his catch, on a large plate with Chinese birds on the rim, down on the table in the front hall. Just as silently, Agnes would collect them from there. I would watch, as the bright spots on the skin of the fish faded, along with the brightness in their eyes. Agnes would groan and mutter to herself as she steered her way down a stone spiral staircase from the hall to the basement corridor.

The reality of my father and mother's transition from what appeared to me to be a 'normal' existence in this lonely cul-de-sac in the Border hills, to somewhere as distant and magical as a fairy tale, was brought home one day when a box arrived from Istanbul, addressed to my two half-brothers. Miss Toye the governess looked on suspiciously as the paper and cardboard wrapping were undone; and she became positively incoherent when four gold dollar pieces were revealed. There were, so my father's memoir recalls, written in 1970 in Corfu when he had settled into his new life far from Scotland and from reminders of the War, two twenty-dollar pieces and two of ten dollars; and he had bought them in mysterious and, as I saw when I read his account, terrifying circumstances. This is what he wrote:

Through a Mr Crabb, who had lived in Turkey for many years, and to whom I had been given a letter of introduction before leaving England, I met Satvet Lufti Tozan, a man of mystery and of apparently enormous wealth. He was, I believe, a Turk, but married to a German wife. He spoke French fluently with a soft and husky voice and lived in a one-time palace on the banks of the Bosphorus. Tozan was anxious to be on intimate terms with me and I well remembered when he invited me and Elizabeth to dine at his house. On arrival at the outer gates we were met by a guard with two huge wolfhounds and conducted to the house itself. Here we were met at the door by Tozan. He was very proud of the fact that after the First World War he had been awarded the OBE for services he had rendered, but he never spoke of what these had been. I suspect that he had been a spy in the British pay – or a double agent. Since then he had developed as a gun runner and supplier of arms with contacts throughout Europe and he was keen to make use of me and the U.K.C.C. if he could. After dinner he took us down to a dimly-lit stone-floored cellar, the far end of which was shut off by an iron grill. It was with some hesitation that I accepted his invitation to follow him through a door in the grill which he unlocked with a heavy key. But we went in only so that he could open a massive safe from which he dragged a sack about three feet high. Cutting a cord he let it fall on its side and a cascade of gold coins poured out onto the floor. They were all ten- or twenty-dollar pieces, and I suppose he showed them to whet my appetite and impress me with his wealth. And it was a sore temptation when he offered me a glittering handful. As it was, I bought and paid for two of the ten- and two of the twenty-dollar pieces, which looked as if they were fresh from the mint. I sent them home to Colin and James.

Of course, my father told this story many times when he was back from the War – but what I hadn't known was the fact that Miss Toye, punctilious to the last, sent the dollar pieces to the Bank of England shortly after their arrival at our house. There had been an appeal by the Government to surrender all gold coins – and the governess was not one to conceal suspicious glittering currency obtained in darkest Turkey.

It came as rather a letdown, after this indication of the extraordinary lives my parents appeared to be leading, to find that life went on much the same day after day at home.

Blackout was rigorously maintained, with May careful not to show even the smouldering tip of a cigarette when she went into the little turret pantry of the nursery to do the washing-up. Agnes, who was a large woman with an air that was melancholy when it was not bad-tempered (though in fact she had a kind nature much misunderstood by those who saw her glowering through the window hatch in the kitchen), produced the meals, and these rattled up to the pantry proper, beyond the dining room, in a lift which appeared to have a mind of its own. Pressing a button to summon the lunch (rabbit, in one of Agnes' many guises, and roly-poly pudding, a strawberry jam sauce succeeding golden syrup as these commodities grew rare in wartime, and cream still often possible, for we were lucky enough to be permitted a cow) often resulted in the entire repast staying stuck midway between floors for an exacerbatingly long time. Sending down the empty dishes later had the frequent result of a satisfying rumble, as if the lift itself was digesting the food, followed by a dash down to the bowels of the house, where a scream could be heard from Bella as shattered plates and glasses bounced in to their destination. We took to washing up in the pantry itself and risked only food and remains in the lift; but the last straw came when a rare piece of sirloin, all that several weeks' food rationing allowed, sat halfway between floors and only emerged cold and congealed when Jimmy's brother, a one-time electrician, had had to squander his petrol allowance by driving from the small town five miles out of our valley.

Agnes achieved many triumphs with the rabbits which abounded in the fields and hills. She made rabbit schnitzel (perhaps something in her Czech background lent her the talent for a deliciously light breadcrumbed escalope of rabbit, which anyone not knowing there was a war on would have considered to be veal) and with the schnitzels she made a bowl of mashed potato with runnels of melted butter (our cow again) that glistened in its folds. There was always a salad of green lettuce from the kitchen garden and small tomatoes from the greenhouse, which tasted sharp and sweet at the same time. But it was only when I was able to spend long periods of time in Greece – that is, a quarter of a century later when the house in Scotland was left for good and a new life for my parents took shape in Corfu – that I learned the sensation of a real, red Mediterranean tomato. Despite their piquancy, the tiny tomatoes from Scotland soon faded from memory, to be replaced by these hand grenades from the sun: infinitely juicy, soft and sweet as the fruit they of course are. I could only admire Agnes in retrospect for combining our glasshouse tomatoes with the few herbs we had dried or grew in the kitchen garden to create the sauce for the rabbit stew which was the most regular alternative to the schnitzels. Once out on the Ionian island where winter rainfall and wooded slopes make as perfect a habitat for rabbits as our own native shores, I understood that large quantities of onions are needed to give the *kounelli stifado* (rabbit stew), so beloved in Corfu, its particularly wonderful and – with a sweetness that comes from the onion as much as it does from the Greek tomato

– unforgettable character. To do Agnes justice, on looking back to those days when an autumnal darkness settled on our house and valley as early as lunchtime and there was no way of knowing whether the War would ever end, her rabbit stews, with their bright colours and subtle flavour (being close to the Hungarians she must have added paprika to everything, much as the Corfiots do), were uplifting in the extreme. After his return from the banks of the Bosphorus, where I imagined the mysterious Tozan pressing a shower of gold coins into his hand at every opportunity, I don't think my father ever liked Agnes' ways with rabbit, for all the efforts she made. But he spoke of the food he and my mother ate in Istanbul, and when I came to Greece I understood that Corfu, although it had repelled Turkish invasions over the centuries, had been almost as heavily influenced as the mainland in its Oriental tastes.

Spring Food

Bright by day, it grows cold in the evenings, and a walk up the grove to search for tiny narcissi followed by a scrunch along a decidedly wintry beach is followed by a warming meal, the colours as bright as the new coat of the assertive robin enjoying the last weeks before the swallows swoop in.

All the dishes in this book are a combination of Maria's village cooking and my mother's suggestions, some from England, France or Scotland. Somehow, and very deliciously, they all taste unmistakably Greek.

Meatballs in Tomato Sauce

Serves 6

for the meatballs:
2 lb / 1 kg minced beef

1 egg

1 tablespoon fresh basil, chopped

½ tablespoon fresh thyme, chopped

1 wineglass fresh parsley, chopped

1 onion, chopped

½ tablespoon fresh mint, chopped

1½ oz / 40 g fresh breadcrumbs

2 tablespoons olive oil

a little milk

salt and black pepper to season

Combine all the ingredients in a bowl, soften with a little milk and knead well with the hands. Leave the mixture to rest in the bowl for two hours, then remove and roll between hands to form sausage shapes of about 4½ inches long, like fingers. Lay in a Pyrex dish.

for the tomato sauce:
1 onion, grated
1 wineglass olive oil
1 basil leaf, chopped
½ teaspoon cinnamon (*canella*)
1 pinch nutmeg
1 bay leaf
250 g tin tomato purée
salt and black pepper to season

In a saucepan, heat the olive oil and fry the onion until golden, then add the bay leaf, basil, cinnamon, nutmeg and season with salt and pepper. Stir in the tomato purée. Cook the ingredients together for two to three minutes, then add two tumblers of water. Bring this to the boil and then reduce to the lowest heat, covering the pan until the sauce has thickened.

Pour the tomato sauce over the meat fingers (don't worry: they will relax into a ball shape in cooking) and place the dish in a medium-hot oven for about half an hour or until the meatballs are cooked all the way through.

Rabbit Stifado

Serves 4

1 rabbit, skinned and gutted
1 small onion, chopped
1 wineglass olive oil
½ teaspoon paprika
1 bay leaf
¾ wineglass vinegar
250 g tin tomato purée
1 lb / 500 g shallots
salt and black pepper to season

Cut the rabbit into evenish pieces, then wash. Put these pieces in a colander and drain them of excess water. Heat the oil in a saucepan and add the chopped onion. Fry until brown. Add the rabbit, paprika and bay leaf, season, and cook for 10–15 minutes over a medium heat.

Now add the vinegar and cook, stirring together for 10 minutes. Next, add the tomato purée diluted with one glass of water. Stir well again, cooking for another 10 minutes.

Prepare the shallots by skinning them and slashing them with a knife across their ends to remove their roots. Add them to the pan and then add some water, pouring down the side of the saucepan until the liquid is level with the meat. Boil rapidly for 10 minutes. Then reduce the heat and — with a lid on — don't stir but shake the pan. Leave to simmer on a low heat until nearly all the liquid has evaporated.

Eat with plenty of fried potatoes.

Yemistes (Stuffed Vegetables)

Serves 6

for the rice:
1 large onion, grated
1 lb / 500 g risotto rice
1 wineglass olive oil
1 tablespoon of tomato purée
2 big handfuls of fresh parsley, chopped
1 teaspoon of fresh or dried thyme
1 tablespoon fresh or dried basil
1 teaspoon fresh mint, finely chopped, or dried
½ teaspoon cinnamon
250 g tin tomato purée

for the vegetables:
2 large tomatoes
2 aubergines
2 green or red peppers
1 wineglass water
1 wineglass olive oil
salt and black pepper to season

In a good-sized saucepan, heat the olive oil over a medium heat and fry the onion. When the onion turns golden, add all the herbs, the seasoning, the tomato purée and one large tumbler of water. Cook for five minutes, then add the risotto rice with another tumbler of water and stir well.

Next, prepare the tomatoes by cutting off their stalk end tops and reserving these. Scoop out half of the flesh, and set aside in a bowl. Now cut around the stalk of the peppers to remove their 'lids', and scrape out the seeds and pith. Cut the aubergines in half lengthwise and remove half of their flesh. Chop the aubergine flesh finely, and place in a bowl with the tomato insides, salt, pepper and a tablespoonful of tomato purée. Add one wineglass of olive oil and a wineglass of water, and mix well with spoon to absorb the purée.

Place the scooped-out vegetable shells close together in an ovenproof dish, 8 inches deep. Fill them with the risotto rice and replace the vegetable lids. Arrange the remaining vegetable flesh mixture around the stuffed vegetables in the dish.

Cook uncovered in a preheated oven at 250 °C / 480 °F for half an hour. Lower heat to 150°C / 300°F, cover with foil and cook for a further half-hour.

Taramasalata is Greece's most famous export after *Never On A Sunday* and resembles that wildly euphoric theme tune: the oil and cod's roe together make an unforgettable starter to lunch or supper.

Taramasalata

1 large onion, grated
juice of 1 large lemon
½ litre / 500 ml olive oil
6 oz / 150 g cod's roe

In a large bowl combine the onion and the roe. Place this in a blender with the lemon juice. As the mixture blends, slowly add the oil as when making mayonnaise.

Greek Easter at Rovinia has a friend, James, running down into the grove with a jug of vodka and tomato juice. He is pulling lemons from the tree in the sunken garden to add to the joy of a Bloody Mary taken sacrilegiously under a flowering Judas, named after Judas Iscariot and thus with blossoms of a blood-red purple, for this is the tree from which the traitor hanged himself in remorse.

We drink – and are glad to rise once more to the terrace, where Thodoros and Maria's children are rolling scarlet eggs and a barbecue of kid or lamb is giving out its strong, smoky smell.

From where we sit, we hear the sounds of a hundred Easter feasts as they take place up in the village. Most of the feasters have eaten little but beans in the last week of Lent, and the joy is almost palpable as it drifts down to us.

Charcoal Grilled Kid or Lamb Chops with Barbecue Sauce

allow 1 lb / 500 g of meat (about four chops) per person
fresh oregano (rigani), chopped
lemon juice
salt and black pepper to season

Prepare the chops in a dish by adding the salt, pepper, oregano and lemon juice. These can be got ready beforehand and left to marinate for a couple of hours.

When the charcoal is ready, place the meat on the grill and cook, turning occasionally for 20–30 minutes. When the meat has turned a good dark colour, take it off the barbecue, transfer to a dish and pour over the following barbecue sauce.

for the barbecue sauce:
Take a large bottle, make holes in the metal lid, then add the following ingredients, shaking thoroughly to mix.

1 small wineglass fresh oregano (rigani), chopped
½ small wineglass fresh rosemary, chopped
1 whole head garlic, skinned and chopped
1 wineglass olive oil
1 wineglass lemon juice
1 wineglass water
salt and black pepper to season

For a long time we weren't let in to the secret of *bourdeto* at Rovinia: it was considered too spicy and too local, perhaps, and it was only after asking if we could share it one day when the sight of the scorpion fish and octopus and the strong aroma of paprika combined with dark, strong Rovinia oil – and of course the *skordo* (garlic) – was too much to resist.

Liapades and the other villages up above the sea have mainly fishermen as inhabitants and, in the case of another Maria, a by-now celebrated fisherwoman. The disappearance of three in a small boat a year back brought fame, TV crews and the final, relieved discovery that all were safe and sound in a cove down the coast – it even had a wood oven.

This fish stew is a real Greek bouillabaisse: rich, burningly hot and chunky.

Bourdeto

Serves 4

4 lb / 2 kg mixed fish (fresh cod, scorpion fish, monk fish, conger eel, octopus — use what is available, but avoid sardines)
1 large onion, coarsely chopped
1 whole head garlic, skinned and chopped
½ coffee-scoop ground black pepper
1 heaped coffee-scoop paprika
2 heaped tablespoons tomato purée
1 wineglass olive oil
salt and black pepper to season

CORFU BANQUET

First scrape all the fish, then wash and gut them. Cut the larger fish into pieces, then place the fish mix in a large, shallow saucepan. To this, add the onion, garlic, black pepper, and paprika.

In a bowl, dilute the tomato purée with a little water, season, and pour this over the fish. Now, add the olive oil, just cover with water and gently shake the saucepan to mix all the ingredients together, but do not stir.

Over a high heat, boil hard for quarter of an hour and then shake the saucepan again. There should not be much water left. Reduce the heat and simmer slowly for about half an hour until the sauce has reduced to a quarter of original.

Serve with green salad and new potatoes.

When the town referred to in this magical dish is Constantinople, the journey of St Spiridon in the saddle-bag of a donkey to reach his island, Kerkyra, is easier to envisage. If saints could be transported with care and determination, so could the receipt which has given so much pleasure over the years – the heart of the artichoke in a dish of purity and miraculous invention.

Anginares Stin Poli (Artichokes of the Town)

Serves 6

8 artichokes, with outer coarse leaves removed and their stalks cut off and set aside, leaving half of the leaves nearest the heart
juice of 1½ lemons
1 lb / 500 g potatoes, peeled and sliced
1 lb / 500 g carrots, peeled and chopped
small bunch of parsley, stalks removed
1 whole head garlic, peeled
1 wineglass olive oil
1 teaspoon black pepper, and salt to taste

Place the artichoke heads in a bowl with the juice of half a lemon to prevent discolouring. Then slice the artichokes vertically as far as the heart and remove the fuzzy part. Cut off the top half of the remaining artichoke leaves. Make an incision on the bases crosswise.

Now throw away the artichokes' lemony water and transfer them, with their peeled stalks, the potatoes and the carrots, to a big saucepan of water with a little salt. Cover the pan, bring to the boil and boil for 3—4 minutes. Pour away half of the water and add the garlic, the juice of one lemon, the parsley, olive oil and black pepper. Cover the pan and boil for 15—20 minutes. Serve either dished up or straight from the pan.

SPRING FOOD

Spring had unusual ways of showing itself on occasion; and the most welcome was always a visit to Rovinia by Marie Aspioti. Despite the (to us) clear signs of hot weather in the offing – we would sit red-armed in T-shirts on the terrace, allowing a raw March sun to burn our pallid skin – Marie stayed in deep-winter garb right up to the summer solstice. I think of her in donkey-brown twinset and small feet shod in a stern leather quite the opposite of our trainers and sandals; and along with the Greek caution over the trickeries of spring sunlight comes the memory of her dry, quick, delightfully nuanced voice, in which interest in everything under the sun is tirelessly evident. Marie, admired and loved by veteran Resistance heroes such as Patrick Leigh Fermor (he would travel to the island simply to spend a day with her), came from an old Corfiot family and lived in a watermelon-red house, battered on the outside, dark and cool within, which we used to pass on drives into the town. She was not rich and must have hated the long hours at a travel agency which she had to put in, when books and ideas and languages were her forte; but she never complained, and used to deal with youngsters totally lost in Corfu with patience and dignity.

As for food, Marie came in her last years to eat nothing more at the Corfu Grill, where she would meet my mother for lunch, than the *gigantes* (butter beans) and a bottle of Sprite, a child-like fizzy drink.

Chapter Four

Swans

The first signs of a real turning of the seasons when it happens at Rovinia take us as always by surprise. For isn't it spring all the year round on this island where we are spending what will possibly turn out to be our last few seasons? My mother has decided to sell this house she and my father built nearly forty years ago; the time has come for us to pull up the roots put down in the years before tourism or even an International Airport. In this wonderful place, which bears the Venetian name for ruins and which yet seems able to renew itself with the same energy as the new cycle of the year, will we ourselves leave any traces? Or shall we simply be a matter of speculation, like the crumbling well with a fig tree sprouting from the depths: was this where the house once was? we say, pausing on a walk up to the terrace where friends once built a hexagonal wooden tower and liked to visit in the heat of summer from their home in Gastouri. Or the lime kiln, down there by the high-water mark on the beach, its original use only visible in the primitive opening to the furnace. Was this where the past owners of our bay once lived, just inches above the detritus brought in by winter storms? Did they know they looked up the sheltered hillside where Odysseus was found by the daughter of the king of the Phaeacians? Could they guess that *xenoi*, foreigners from a northern country, would come to Rovinia and enjoy the olive grove that must always have provided shade for walking down to the sea?

The time has come to leave Rovinia and a brochure has been printed, which shows the terraces and the long room with the vaulted ceiling that leads out to a view no one ever forgets who sees it: an expanse of blue Ionian sea, a promontory like a hedgehog's snout and a cave which looks as if it has been drawn onto the hill opposite with a charcoal pencil. There are pictures of olive trees – a handful of the ten million the Venetians caused to be planted on the island so their city would never go short of oil – and there are shots of the beach from many angles. In one of these, very faint, two figures side by side on the new sand brought in by last year's storm are myself and my mother, snapped by Tim. They have been airbrushed out by the designer to give an inaccurate impression of the total solitude and privacy considered a requisite of the luxurious way of life. Privacy on Greek beaches, apart from being an unusual commodity, is illegal if enforced by an individual owner's construction of fence or gate. Up to high-water mark, the beach is public property.

So we are ghosts in our own demesne, erased from the land where for thirty-five years we have watched the flowers grow and lain in the still water green as chrysopahase or tourmaline and seen the sea jewels: coloured glass polished by the waves to form necklaces against the sand and stones underwater. Our absence won't be noticed, certainly, by the tribe of long-legged birds which comes each spring, stilts as they are called, delicate as small flamingos, round-shouldered and like a group of resting, hesitant overseas visitors by the edge of the sea. They pause here on their way north from Africa, and we tiptoe at the far end of the beach for fear of disturbing a rest taken after hours of flight. Like the swallows, which have just started to arrive: dark blue flashes in the olives before flying up to their nests in the verandah like written promises of a faithful return to old haunts, the stilts are clearly not strangers to this bay. The worry comes: will the next inhabitants respect these visitors (memories of a renter of the house who scoured the rafters with a long broom and thus removed the swallows' long-accustomed nesting places come bitterly to mind)? Will a billionaire build a marina or a harbour in imitation of the ancient Greeks and scare the shy, huddled stilts away from this perfect temporary sanctuary?

The answer, of course, cannot be known; and although we have sworn that we will not sell to a developer intent on putting up hotels and swimming pools at Rovinia, who knows what will happen in the end? The best and only course is to read of other habitats for the birds who come in spring – the salty marshland loved by the stilts and the broken-down farm buildings in deserted rural areas (and there are many of these) where the swallows, if our house is no longer available to them, will be able to build undisturbed.

I'm up on the terrace one morning after a fit of these gloomy thoughts, and I see the binoculars, an old pair of my father's which have miraculously survived raids by young children on the cupboard in the sitting room as well as rising storms at sea when our big caique, the *Falaina* (meaning whale), was still in use, are lying on the balustrade. Like the fateful objects in *Alice in Wonderland*, they invite examination; and although it's obvious that Tim has spent the last hours scanning the virgin Mediterranean forest across our narrow valley for golden oriole, finch or jay, I am unable to resist picking up the glasses, going down to the beach and adjusting the sight to meet my own increasingly faulty vision. At first, as always seems to happen when I try out these ancient binoculars made by the enticingly named and now defunct Negretti & Zamba of Mayfair in London, the sudden rush of the stones on the beach a hundred feet away is alarming, not to say disorientating. Which part of the dried-out riverbed have I landed in? Surely this can't be our familiar beach, with pebbles magnified absurdly and a colony of large birds visible, paddling in shallow, pale water? It might as well be the surface of the moon or a still from *Jurassic Park*, with pterodactyls about to take off into the dawn of time.

As if aware of being stared at through these sportsmen's lenses, the stilts (for this of course they are) rise suddenly of one accord and fly gracefully north, in the direction of Paleocastritsa Bay. I curse to myself, for if I'd left well alone we might have enjoyed hours or days more of their magical visit. But then, as if to compensate for my clumsiness, the other birds come into view. And when I call out to Tim to share my excitement and realise he must, unusually for him, have left the glasses on the balustrade before going on one of his long walks to the surrounding villages of Gardelades or Doukades, there is nothing for it but to run up to the terrace in search of Thodoros. I need a witness to this manifestation of a new pageant of the spring.

Two swans sail out at sea, as white and trim as sailing boats (but even with my lack of expertise in the use of binoculars I can see quite plainly that these are not ships; they are swans). In my despondent state of thoughts of the future of the valley and the grove, of the primaeval site where the house stands – and this we have decided it must be, for it lies right in the path of the setting sun on the mountain's saddle across the bay, at the time of spring and autumn equinox – in my state of anxiety and dejection, I can't help seeing the swans as true harbingers of hope. Indeed, of another spring: swans, as far as I know, are not commonly seen right out at sea like this. Calm weather must lie ahead. All will go smoothly with the sale of Rovinia; it will remain just the same, cherished and loved. It will always be the bay three miles south of the palace of King Alcinous at Paleocastritsa, where Homer states that King

Odysseus encountered the *Bora* wind which blew his craft over and sent it to the bottom of the sea. In the soap-opera scene which follows this drama, Odysseus finds himself stranded in the bay where the beautiful Princess Nausicaa, daughter of King Alcinous, and her maidens happen to be washing linen, brought all the way from Paleocastritsa. After hiding behind an olive branch, Odysseus appears to the princess, who offers him the stunning hospitality of her father's palace with its year-round fruit garden and magically lit banqueting halls. (We've often hoped to hear that foundations have come to light; but a wooden construction of mythical origin would be hard to find.)

'*Plastiki.*' Thodoros has heard my excited call and stands behind me. He doesn't need binoculars to see the white birds floating on the surface of the water beyond our promontory. And he goes on to explain that these artificial birds are used as decoys – though I can't understand what for. That they aren't real is enough for me, at present; and it takes a walk in the grove and the sight of the new poppies, pricked red in the sandy arms of the estuary formed by last winter's storms, to restore my faith in the everlastingness of nature, Greece and our legendary bay. No amount of plastic swans, I promise myself, will alter this beautiful landscape.

However, as I was to discover later when the birds could be seen in real close up down in the tiny, sunless bay behind the house, they weren't 'plastic' at all. It was a Greek idea of a joke.

Chapter Five

Corfu Blue

It's always good to find a reason for visiting Corfu Town: for me, at least, it's a magical doll's house, with brightly coloured fruit and vegetables piled all year round on barrows outside shops as dark and small as when they were first built, in the age of Venetian supremacy or under the French at the time of the Revolution. I see, too, the jewellers I visited with my daughters when they were very young and dreamed of rings, bracelets and dangling hoops of gypsy gold for ears painfully pierced at far too early an age.

'*Oxi*,' the old man in the musty shop down by the port says, as we pore over trays where the sinister blue eye of the Greek warding-off-evil ring lies amongst ancient cornelians and a dark signet ring, the stamp long grown invisible in the centuries of changing history since a young noble from San Marco discarded it amongst his olive groves at Gouvia.

'*Oxi*,' as we hold out to him the Aladdin's cave contents of years' beachcombing at Rovinia: emerald glass, white shards from long-disintegrated bottles and the occasional deep blue of a real Venetian goblet, swept into our high-water mark in a freak storm one day. But the old man says these treasures can't be strung together on a filigree chain, as we have asked, to wrap around the girls' necks, or to weave in hair, a sea-tiara. The remnants would disintegrate, and we'll take them home again, to live in the pottery bowl on the mantelpiece. It was a waste of time, to bring them; but the shopkeeper, who reveals suddenly a tray of tiny turquoise rings, sees his chance, and pudgy fingers leave the shop adorned with these other marine-shaded gems, each set in a band of murky gold.

No one would dream of leaving for home without going in to pay respects to St Spiridon, great survivor of the Second World War, as well as several major and unsuccessful invasions by Turks, not to mention his own journey with St Theodora to Kerkyra in the first place.

The Italians, given the go-ahead by the Germans in 1940 to bomb Corfu, used the town as target practice. Tragic accounts of those who sheltered in a school near the great church and their dreadful deaths combine with breathless wonder at the miracle performed by the saint: in all the carnage and destruction of the lovely town, the church remained unharmed. We'll go up the steps, beyond the pious-kitsch shops, after tasting a good cappuccino in the little piazza where The Body Shop, glaringly English with its soaps and loofahs, strikes the only discordant note. I will say Hurry Up, we're meeting Granny at Aegli for lunch and we've still to look for the powder-paint place, and pigeons will scatter as we make our entrance into the deep gold, incense-scented interior.

'Is that really St Spiridon?' a child will want to know, for she understands him only as the small bronze statue at Rovinia applied to with varying degrees of urgency, if a storm and an incoming plane with a guest or family member, as so often, are coinciding – or, more usually, if plumbers and electricians simply cannot be found at times of flood or power-cut. 'Why is he small? How can he fit in that box?' The saint lies in a catafalque, resting in the interlude between his Easter appearances – and on his feast day, too, he is drawn through the streets, the great bearded *pappases* walking solemnly in his cortège. It is indeed easy to believe the bombers of the last World War were somehow daunted by this tiny figure.

The blue of the powder paint I seek – it's to be found at certain ironmonger shops, but these are getting harder to locate – is the blue of the Virgin's heavenly robe, the blue of saints and the Madonna, who is said to have thrown her cloak over a bush on the island, so the flowers of the rosemary turned blue. I need to replenish my store in London, where a room that had been a dingy basement has been transformed by this paint, dragged over white emulsion. (The powder must be mixed to a paste first, with water, and then added to white, as strong or pale as one wants it.) This is the bright, candid blue of village houses, and there's a chrome yellow and a terracotta that can also be bought, ladled from huge sacks and weighed, sold for the modern euro equivalent of a few drachmas. And while the other colours are good, the blue transcends all else.

I breathe a sigh of relief when we've found the store with its shelves of hooks and nails and brushes and walked down a slope in this steep, pretty mostly Venetian city to the great open ground bordered by the arcades of the Liston. Just a few minutes late – and my mother can easily be seen, braving an outdoor table at Aegli, one of the town's oldest restaurants and protected by grey stone arches from a sudden downpour.

Cherry trees in full blossom border the green expanse where cricket, legacy of British occupation right through the middle of the nineteenth century, is played; and beyond lies the sea, as blue as the precious powder secreted in my bag. The girls show their rings, and an ancient, child-friendly waiter brings ouzo and Coca-Cola. After lunch we'll go looking for the statue of the brave Austrian general in the employ of the Venetians, John Schulenburg, who repulsed the last invasion of 3,300 Turks in 1716. Then, perhaps, the small museum, where a frieze of Dionysus drinking wine at a stone table is oddly modern in feel as the charming god looks down at his innocent young companion.

The food at Aegli is good – I choose fish and the children like *pastitsia*, a Corfiot version of macaroni pie. But it doesn't compare, we all agree, with Maria's cooking. And we'll drive home in the new Hyundai, astonished afresh at the landscape created by Spiro the builder's road.

Chapter Six

Lentils to Easter

In the days when my father was alive and we still had the *Falaina*, 'the big caique', a splendidly solid vessel which could sleep two in the cabin with another up on deck, the most certain sign of approaching summer was its arrival at the end of our small jetty by the entrance to the cave. All the small craft bobbing in the waves made by the *Falaina*'s majestic approach were like toy boats, as collapsible as children's bathtime playthings in comparison with the Lister-engined thirty-metre-long seafaring fishing-boat constructed in the harbour of the old port in Corfu Town. She could take us as far as Italy, if we so wished; we could sleep, cook in the galley kitchen, and (as so often promised to ourselves and as regularly not accomplished due to oversleeping and laziness) rise at five in the morning to test Homer's veracity in describing the rosy-fingered dawn.

Since the great invasion of tourists on the island it has become a new and just as accurate an indication of the change in season to see a caique almost identical to our long-lost *Falaina*. The *Falaina* was sold by my mother after my father's death; an event which found amongst prospective buyers the local wide-boys who, in return for what they hoped would be a bargain, came to make their offer with bags of oranges and lemons as a gift (though their expectations of doing a sharp deal with a poor widow were, unfortunately for them, scuppered).

The large caiques ply up and down the west coast, generally leaving from Paleocastritsa or Yefira Bay and going down as far as Ermones, past the glorious bay at Iliodorus where my mother and sister, going down there in the small *Falaina* still gather samphire and wild fennel (*marathra*) for our summer salads. Music blares from the tourist caiques as they go by, and we know the summer is well underway if they come in to dock in our bay, where storms brought by the south wind can get up quickly and make departure impossible. It's not difficult to imagine an assortment of Danes, Brits and Swedes camped in the grove and depending on the wood fires they build to make their kebabs for as long as the wind blows – and their being there wouldn't matter if it weren't for the love of loudspeakers indulged by the organisers of the group. It's as if, so a visiting archaeologist remarks, these booming voices belong to an archaic landscape, so little else has changed in the woodland, rocky coves and deserted stretches of the still unspoilt west coast. It was with a voice as loud as this, our lunching visitor tries to cheer us, that a sailor on Paxos, the island to the south of Corfu, broadcast to the world the news of the death of the great god Pan.

But the very existence of the big caique tied up by our little pier, its mast sticking up so it looks as if it's right at the end of our own table on the verandah, gives us boatsick thoughts, if such an expression can be said to exist. We are remembering the picnics Maria used to make: the cold rice salad glistening in its dressing of olive oil and lemon juice, red and green peppers and tomato giving a sharp, nutty taste when eaten with chicken and the mayonnaise Thodoros liked to make, a sauce as deep yellow as the sun overhead. We sit for a time in silence, while our good-natured guest expounds on the typical Greekness of the scene we find ourselves in, on this day of the mass-tourist picnic beneath us on the beach and the megaphone instructions of the guides. 'The Mediterranean sense of eternity,' he says gently – and it's true, little could compare to this early summer day, a sky of uninterrupted blue, a faint breeze, the new sprouting of the lovely, forested hill across our olive-filled valley all give a sense of such a day repeated as unendingly as the long shafts of patterned silver in the changing sea beyond – 'the sense of eternity that exists in Greece is and always has been punctuated by interruptions. It is what provides the ironic interaction of the country.' And we all laugh, reconciled at last to the crowds and their music below.

'The storms, the plumbing disasters,' we spell out, and summoning up the times of a day of equal perfection takes us back to reality with a sudden, drastic power-cut or a furious thunderstorm appearing in the skies above Lakones. It was life in Greece, we remind ourselves, that showed us there is no such thing as a perfect, unchanging day. And, ironically, these whims or thunderbolts make this the most perfect country to live in the world.

If we are still far from adept at second-guessing the gods or the weather, Maria seems to know instinctively which way the wind is going to blow. Surprising us on a grey, chilly morning with the announcement that today is '*poli zesti*' – very hot, Maria is proved right an hour or so later when a new heat comes into the sun's rays, and we start throwing off long-sleeved T-shirts and deciding to risk the cold water of the bay, after all. If we do don bathing-suits and go down steps bordered by rosemary and broom pushing bright from under the *stoa* (the basement of our house, which from below looks like a fortified rampart), she is the first to remind us that she herself takes to the sea only in *megalo kalokairi* (high summer). And that is a long way off. Even the sight of a kingfisher flashing bright blue and green over the rocks on the point beyond our wing, or *xenona* (guest house), doesn't warm us until we've gone in and built an olive-wood fire. And still, even after that, we need Maria's cooking to warm us completely. *Spada*, shoulder of lamb, cooked to Maria's secret – and surprising – recipe, sits in a pool of richly caramelised onions. Potatoes that are firm and sweet and soft lie alongside the meat in a big pottery dish. (I've come to believe that the best potatoes in the Mediterranean world must come from Corfu; but then the *cremidia* (onions) in all their different guises, are incomparable too.) Separately, *kokinogouli*, one of the countless species of greens found plentifully here, this one of a beet variety, make a wonderful vegetable. And, a sure sign that spring has met early summer and the sea must soon realise this and warm to the increasing heat of the sun, a dish of wild strawberries comes afterwards, delicious with a froth of just-whipped cream.

The spring equinox has passed and the wait to Greek Easter, late this year, has never seemed longer. We follow some of Maria's Lenten diet – but cheating sometimes, when the soups and cheese we promise ourselves aren't enough in the cool evenings. But there are so many new-season treats that we don't need to leave a diet that is almost exclusively vegetarian: for who, however hungry, could fail to be satisfied by *spanakorisi*, a dream of spinach and rice and tomato, a soupy substance that is half risotto and half a rich soup? And which of us, seeing the tiny new artichokes, can forget the last time this herald of a long April and May, the almost chokeless *anginari* came onto the table? For all that the Turks never succeeded in conquering Corfu, the dish best known on the island in these spring and early summer months is *anginares stin poli*, and although the lentil soup made by Maria and eaten nightly does fortify against chilly evenings and the aftermath of foolhardy bathes, no supper is as delicate and satisfying as artichokes as once they were cooked on the shores of the Bosphorus.

And finally Greek Easter comes at last, and the weather is suddenly lovely too – we bathe in water where the sun makes threads of gold in the shifting blues and greens of the sea: 'It's the first Good Friday anyone can remember when the candles in the midnight procession weren't blown out by the wind,' Maria says.

Chapter Seven

Mountains

I'm standing in the nursery of our house in Scotland and I know lunch is ready, but I'm not able to go down and tuck into Agnes' rabbit stew and bread-and-butter pudding because a strange man is attacking the table with a hammer – and as he does so, fragments of bright, brittle toffee fly up in the air and then fall to the ground and turn to dust. I know that May will be furious when she sees what needs to be cleaned up and I fight back my tears: it would be humiliating to be found sobbing over something that was clearly intended as a treat for me alone. As well as that, I am now five years old and have a reputation, in the absence of my parents because of the War, for being a tomboy, even a runaway. I've escaped to Innerleithen, the nearest small town a good five miles away, with a friend, Anne, whom I persuaded to join me in the pursuit of ice cream (there is an Italian ice cream parlour there, as there were in so many Scottish towns at the time, and the highly artificial raspberry ripple is my heart's desire). I've set up camp alone with a village friend on the island in the middle of Loch Eddy at the end of the valley, and I've joined in ratting expeditions above the byre in the farm when May and anyone else who happened to be in this curious mock-castle in the years of avoiding German bombs thought me fast asleep. So I mustn't cry now, when Derek Hill, a friend of my mother's and a painter (later he will produce a picture of Corfu but this has disappeared somewhere in family moves), attacks the sheet of hard, caramelised sugar lying on the thick fabric of the William Morris cloth in the nursery. I see the stitched pheasants and the berries on the branches of the trees where the birds perch, as the tapestry cloth goes under Derek's hammer; and I know, dimly, that there will be trouble when it's discovered what a beating this ancient relic of my grandmother's love affair with Morris, Burne-Jones et al has undergone. Why is Derek, whose last attempt at a sugary concoction took the form of cloudberry jelly (I still resent the long walk in mist and rain across the tops of hills and down the cleuch to pick these grey-beigeish berries, Derek exulting and my mother secretly searching for mushrooms – fox mushrooms, as Mrs McKay calls them, chanterelles to my mother – under the odd clump of silver birch or beechwood), why is Derek so intent on producing a masterpiece here when Agnes does so well with her roly-poly puddings and castle cakes, adding hot raspberry jam when the golden syrup is no longer findable at Ray Martin's shop in town? Does he hope to return to those pre-war days I can barely remember, except for the bright little granules May used to put on my bread for tea: hundreds and thousands, soon swallowed up by wartime strictures and now not even available on a sweet ration? Is Derek, as he smashes into the impossible sheet of toffee, trying to show me what those glorious days were like? Must he now, as he surely does, laugh and say he'll try fudge next time and he'll make it dark and crumbly? It takes an effort to run down the passage to the top of the stairs and call for May – for I know this sticky mess must not be left to glue itself a minute longer to the tablecloth. But I do; and soon everyone is running up to the nursery and I feel somehow to blame, though it all ends in laughter. Derek appears unrepentant, even annoyed with the toffee for having been so recalcitrant. He says he'll make a bilberry fool tomorrow – until someone says the small, purple berries that grow so profusely on our Scottish hills are really better eaten just on their own, their nearly bitter tang giving a clear taste of moor, game bird and craggy heather.

When years later the life in Scotland came to an end, it wasn't just the discoveries here and there of the remains of British occupation in Corfu – the British were on the island in the high-Victorian days which saw the building of my great-grandfather's turreted showplace, and a plethora of bread puddings in island cuisine show an influence I remember from the War, when Agnes' currants and glistening, milky bread-and-butter pudding was worth knowing about in advance so as to leave room for many helpings – it was a sense of solitary lives and bravery that took me back to the time we first came to the west of Corfu and my parents settled there to live. Like the Scots, the Corfiots who lived in the valleys or on the slopes of the high hills and mountain ranges, from Pantocrator to Castel Sant Angelo, had suffered cold and deprivation and enemy attacks for centuries. They lived simply, and their eyes had a clear, direct gaze. In the case of the inhabitants of the chain of villages near and above Rovinia – Gianades, Doukades and Liapades – it was easy to believe that any one village could hear anything said in a neighbouring village without the slightest difficulty, so loud were people's voices; and I would think of Jimmy as he walked the hills, gun across his arm, and how the sound of his loud and clear command of his dogs came right down the side of the mountain, as far as the walled kitchen garden and the path back to the house. The bright, cold air on autumn and spring days in Greece and Scotland seemed alike to me, on this Ionian island where there are forty days of rainfall after the middle of October, and wild cyclamen and crocus push up on high ground like the bilberries, cranberries and cloudberries of our northern home. And I found, when my father wrote of his exploits as head of SOE Cairo (Special Operations Executive) in the War, that the mountains of Greece had indeed provided the heroes of the Resistance to the Germans and that my father, brave himself in his rebellion against the decrees of Winston Churchill, had done all he could in turn to save them.

When my father wrote his memoir of fourteen months in Cairo from 1942, he included the letters of thanks from the leaders of the Resistance groups, most of them Communists, for organising their flight from the mountains of Epirus and Mount Parnassus to Cairo to discuss their continued effort against the Germans. They were warmly greeted and taken to a safe house to talk, along with Mr Leeper, the British Ambassador: but the next day Leeper denied that he had met the Resistance organisers and backed out of his promises of support. The reason lay in Churchill's determination to have the king of Greece restored to the throne once the War was over; and the Resistance Groups were of course Republican and strongly against a restoration of the monarchy in Greece. For a time, the leaders, stranded in Cairo, were in considerable danger, and it was only as a result of my father's efforts that they were flown back to their mountain hide-outs. These efforts cost my father his job, and by the middle of 1943 he was back in Scotland. Nearly thirty years later, when Rovinia was built and he lived permanently in Greece, my father looked around with some anxiety for a place to conceal the letters of thanks from the Resistance leaders – for the Colonels had seized power and no one was safe from their actions or decisions. One day I heard wood as it was sawed vigorously in the vicinity of the sunken garden at Rovinia – but whether the sincere expressions of gratitude from the movements ELAS, EKKE and EAM now push up the wild lilies or spreading rosa mundi planted down there by my mother, I do not know.

What is certain is that these letters were important to my father, and proved his independence of spirit and love of justice, for he preferred losing his post as head of SOE in Cairo to condoning the unfair treatment of the Resistance group leaders by the British under Churchill.

Chapter Eight

High Summer

A new light and a new bounce come into the sky and sea. It's sudden, yet it must have been gradual, this transformation from spring to summer, because the poppies down on the beach are still small and signalling there's plenty of time yet before a baking heat whisks them and all traces of greenery in the grove into a dusty plain. Surely, we think as the brightness gathers strength and eyes begin to ache for rest after midday, we're still only in June?

But it's not only the plants that mark the rise of high summer; it's the people, careening down the heavens in vast kite-shaped balloons or cutting the water into tilled furrows of foam as they zoom back and forth in Boston whalers, speed-trikes, sea-scooters of every description. All at once, the landscape is frightening, even dangerous: what became of the woman seen swimming out and turning into Yefira Bay with long, satisfied strokes? Was she decapitated by the mini-Triton dancing over from a nosy yacht to stare at the house and the beach before gliding on to Ermones? Won't the small craft, some still not equipped with the radios or mobiles recently made mandatory, be swamped by the wash of the big boats or simply run into the side of the cliff?

When the first caique of tourists from the Cricketer's Hotel in the next bay finally proclaimed the irreversible start of summer, my father would sit back in his chair at the head of the long table on the verandah and roll his eyes. Music ('pop' as he had heard it called by his children but, like a High Court Judge, refused so to term it himself) blared from loudspeakers as the big caiques unloosed their cargo onto the beach. A cloud of black smoke, encouraged with petrol and fire-lighters, rose from the barbecue. Some visitors, already as good as naked, rushed into the sea with bottles to cool the wine in what was already warm water. My mother, determined to see the bright side, would remark at this point that she had been applied to again to permit an electric connection to run from our house to the beach, so that visitors could cook their own hamburgers – or set up stalls to sell them – and that the permission had been and would always be refused. This should have been reassuring, but her words were possibly inaudible due to the level of noise blasting into the natural amphitheatre formed by hills and shore at Rovinia. The long and short of it, so my father's back view seemed to say as he went purposefully off to his studio to paint, was that this was pretty unbearable and the absence of a power point wouldn't make much difference.

People, their presence or absence, have always been an important part of the Greek landscape. Moonlight on our beautiful bay looks distinctly different if, as happened one summer, twenty Finnish policemen have decided to camp out on the beach all night. Their bonfire and songs may have brought the days of the ancients to mind, but the revelling until the early hours almost brought on a nostalgia for the sound of the Blue Grotto Bar and its Rolling Stones selections, just by the entrance to Paleocastritsa Bay. And the fact that morning will in all probability bring the raucous tones of the row between the 'chair lady', an ancient from the village with a pile of precarious loungers to rent out at exorbitant prices, and the middle-aged man with his roots in Scandinavia who has decided to provide competition, is hardly comforting. Where is the silence and repose to be hoped for in the perfect setting of a Greek island?

The answer, of course, is that we are spoilt by the quiet Rovinia gives us at most times: the peep of the scops owl and its occasional mate from the wild olive groves on the forested hill across the valley from our house; the soft splash of water on the shingle, which makes me listen for porpoises or smugglers – anything to interrupt the regularity of the waves. And in the mornings the soft, drawn-out dialect of the swallows can hardly be described as disturbing. We are lucky to live almost all the time out of our own time and are glad to remember this.

We're going up and up and little Spiro's ears are popping as we climb in the wonderful new car to his father's restaurant, high in the clouds. Aptly-named 'Paradise', the taverna is perched on the most awkward vertical corner imaginable, on the twisting road up to Trompetta – and arrival there clearly needs to be earned with teeth-gritting and gear-grinding, even prayer.

But it's well worth the visit – the view is quite magnificent, with both sides of the island visible from huge plate-glass windows and a terrace to the side where eucalyptus trees provide shade in high summer. We've been early in the year, and stared out at all the villages we know so well which surround us like a string of beads: Gardelades, Doukades, Gianades and Liapades itself on a high hill opposite, houses and hidden courtyards minute as a toy community. We tell Maria and Thodoros, over a fine Greek lunch of *souvlaki* and chips, that we've visited Gianades this morning before coming here and are impressed by the new *plateia* and the flowers that sprout from every balcony and window-sill. But a woman at the next table is unimpressed. 'They live like animals in Gianades,' she remarks.

High Summer Food

What is best to eat on those high summer evenings when the heat lies over everything and refuses to depart when night falls?

The antique world shrank from eating basil (they claimed it grew at the entrance to the Underworld as a reminder to the newly dead of the beauty of the world they left behind and would not cook with it), but basil in the form of home-grown pesto, made from the small curly-leafed variety in our pots at the end of the terrace, is unbeatable on a hot summer night. With pasta and *graviera* cheese (a Greek Gruyère, as the name suggests) grated on top, this is what the body and the palate need in extreme conditions. And pears in red wine later, with a dollop of fresh yoghurt, is a dish that cools and calms as well.

It should be added here that we don't have pine nuts (and I've no idea why) in the Corfiot pesto as do the Italians. The strong, tiny basil leaves provide all the flavour we need, and Maria's pesto sauce is the strongest, most vivid and aromatic basil sauce imaginable. But, when asked, Maria agrees that eating tagliatelle or noodles with this sauce belongs strictly to Italy and not to Corfu.

Pesto Sauce

1 whole head garlic
1 wineglass olive oil
1 wineglass water
1 ¼ wineglass fresh basil

Put the peeled cloves of garlic in a blender with one wineglass of water. Whizz until smooth. Then remove the stalks from the basil and add the leaves to the blender with the olive oil.

This sauce is best eaten fresh, poured over pasta.

Pears in Red Wine

Serves 10

10 pears
red wine
2 wineglasses caster sugar
1 ½ teaspoons cinnamon

Peel the pears and place them in a saucepan with the sugar, the cinnamon and enough red wine to cover.

Boil until the pears are soft, then remove the fruit and set aside in a serving dish. Reduce the wine sauce over a medium-high heat until thickened and pour over the pears.

Heat dazzles and melts, and this ratatouille, with its herbs, tomatoes and oil, is just right for a lunch outdoors before the sun creeps through the pillars of the verandah and drives everyone in to lie comatose. A July and August treat, easy to make and as forgettable by evening as a siesta dream.

Easy Ratatouille

Serves 6

1 tin chopped tomatoes in their juice
2 large aubergines
2 lbs / 1 kg onions
1 green and 1 red pepper
1 lb / 500 g courgettes
1 teaspoon fresh mint, chopped
1 tablespoon fresh oregano (rigani), chopped
1 bay leaf
1 large wineglass olive oil
salt and black pepper to season

Simply chop up the vegetables and throw them into a baking tin. Season with salt and pepper.

Pour over the tomatoes, their juice and the oil and bake in a very hot oven for about an hour, stirring the ratatouille two or three times whilst it cooks so that the top vegetables do not catch and burn. Eat with bread or rice.

In the evenings of the summer solstice when the paragliders have floated away into the dying light and even the 'bronze goddess', as our most frequent beach-visitor has come to be known, is safely back in her hotel, this is a dish which celebrates the wonderful qualities of spinach. Both a soup and a main course – and to be eaten when the best spinach is still fresh and abundant in town and countryside.

Spinach Rice

Serves 4

2 lbs / 1 kg spinach, chopped, washed and pre-boiled for two minutes
13 oz / 320 g risotto rice
1 onion, chopped
1 tin chopped tomatoes
½ wineglass of olive oil
salt and pepper to season

In a pan, brown the onion in the oil, and then add the tomatoes. Season. Transfer to a saucepan and add the spinach and three litres of water. Stir all the ingredients together, and when water boils add the risotto rice. Boil for 20 minutes (not too fast), then turn the heat down very low and cook, stirring frequently, until the water is absorbed.

My father's distrust of garlic lasted long into his years in Greece. '*Skordo*,' we whispered to each other if a salad had clearly received a dose of the forbidden bulb. *Skordalia* was not mentioned at all, for reasons that will become clear on reading Maria's recipe.

We ate *skordalia* often, with roast chicken or with fish, amused each time that so innocuous mashed-potato-appearing a concoction could blast us sky-high with the sheer intoxication of garlic. Best in summer, when the skin's pores sweat it out.

Skordalia

Serves 6

2 lbs / 1 kg potatoes
2 whole heads garlic
juice of 1 lemon
½ wineglass water
1 wineglass olive oil
salt

Peel the potatoes and cut them into small pieces. Boil until soft in salted water. Drain.

Soak the bulbs of garlic in tepid water, then remove their skins. Chop finely, then transfer to a blender with the lemon juice and water. Add a little salt and liquidise.

In a bowl, mash the potatoes into a purée, then add the garlic mixture. Very slowly, add the oil to the potato until you gain a soft consistency — about one wineglass of oil.

Even at the height of the summer season, *sofrito* is a must, by reason of its intriguing taste and glistening appearance. A Corfiot speciality, *sofrito* features on TV, and competitions and prizes are woven around this wonderful dish. For a lunch party but not for a picnic, as the sauce must not congeal.

Sofrito

Serves 6

12 slices of beef, tender meat: slices from the leg or sirloin
steak, beaten flat
1½ wineglasses olive oil
a little plain flour
1 whole head garlic, chopped
3 wineglasses fresh parsley, chopped
2 wineglasses red wine
1 sprig of fresh rosemary, leaves chopped
1 teaspoon white wine vinegar
salt and pepper to season

Cut the beef slices in half and coat both sides in flour. In a frying pan, heat the oil until very hot. Add the beef and fry for two minutes on each side, then transfer to a saucepan and set aside. To the oil in the frying pan, add the garlic and parsley and cook for a couple of minutes, then add the red wine. Boil gently until reduced to a third.

Pour the red-wine sauce over the beef. Add water, pouring down the saucepan's side until the meat is just covered. Transfer to a high heat, and boil vigorously for five minutes. Turn down the heat to very low, and add the rosemary. Do not stir, just shake the saucepan.

Cook on this low heat for half an hour, or perhaps longer if the meat is tough, checking often to ensure that the sauce has not dried up, and adding more water if necessary. Shake the pan often, about four or five times.

The dish is ready when the sauce has thickened and the meat is cooked through and tender.

Summer, and the sea is so blue when the *Maestro* wind blows from the north, that it's hard to remember how rough the white horses round the sides of the cliffs can become; and how our big caique used to strain in choppy seas as we clung to the hatch where our picnic had been laid out.

Cold chicken; rice salad with peppers and tomatoes; but best of all, if the fishing was successful that day, *sinegrida* (a kind of *loup de mer*) or even swordfish – though this was most likely to be found in the town, not caught by us – for supper later.

This sauce to accompany the swordfish can be used on *papallini*, another Venetian word for the fish that are tinier than whitebait, or on sardines: it is astringent, cool and delicious, and we'll have it with the wild samphire too, when we find it on a trip out by boat.

Swordfish and Salamura Sauce

Serves 4

2 large swordfish steaks, about 3 lbs / 1½ kg each

for the salamura sauce:
4 tablespoons olive oil
juice of 1 large lemon
a couple of pinches fresh oregano (rigani), chopped
2 tablespoons water
salt and pepper to season

The salamura sauce should be ready when the fish comes out of the frying pan, so make this first by putting all the sauce ingredients into small jam-jar, securing the lid and mixing by shaking thoroughly. Next, cut each swordfish steak in two and wash and lightly salt the *fish, draining for half an hour to get rid of excess water. The steaks can be grilled or fried.*

If frying, heat about 1 inch depth of olive oil in a frying pan over a medium heat. Flour the fish lightly on both sides, then place them in the pan for 10 minutes each side, to colour them only slightly. Do not allow them to brown.

If grilling, dust the fish with a little chopped oregano and black pepper and grill for about 10 minutes on each side under a medium grill.

Transfer the steaks to a large serving plate and pour over the cold salamura sauce.

When my father died, the big caique was put up for sale, but it seemed for a time that no one would want to buy the lovely fishing-boat which had taken us all far out to sea and into the unsuspecting bays of unvisited and uninhabited islands. We would never find a buyer, at any price … but then, when the summer came and the season of figs and melons was upon us, a real future owner of the *Faleina* appeared.

We were sorry to see her go; but with summer puddings like these, we were compensated for the loss.

Figs in Syrup

Serves 3

6 figs

for the syrup:
½ pint / 300 ml water
¾ wineglass caster sugar
½ wineglass maraschino

Cut the figs into halves or quarters, as preferred. Now make the syrup. In a pan, add the sugar to the water and heat gently to dissolve the sugar, without boiling. Remove from the heat, and pour in the maraschino, stir once and add the figs to marinate. Cool thoroughly before serving on plates with whipped cream or Greek yoghurt, or a mixture of both.

Stuffed Melon

Serves 6

1 large melon, any variety is good
2 lbs / 1 kg seedless green grapes, halved
3 figs, peeled and cut into halves or quarters

Cut off the top of the melon to make a 'lid' for the fruit. Scoop out the melon's flesh with a spoon. Chop into bite-able pieces and mix together in a bowl with the grapes and figs. Fill the melon shell with the fruit mix, replace the lid, and place in refrigerator for two hours or more before serving with some Greek yoghurt.

High summer with its sea of an impossible blue brought one year an artist, Clotilde Peploe, to Rovinia; and I have associated ever since that one visit in July with the highest period of summer. Maybe it's because Clotilde's paintings, which are often of cliffscapes and marine scenes in the Cycladic islands of Serifos or Folegandros, capture the essence of heat: the lizard peninsulas of ancient grey stone, the stubby vegetation, the sun like Cyclops' eye staring down balefully from the middle of a universe that looks as if it must stay blue forever. It's the only time of year – if you're looking out to sea, at least – when some of that sheer blueness and rocky aridity can be seen in Corfu. Look inland, of course, and the olive groves, cypresses and wonderful greenness – even at the time of St Spiridon's birthday in August – is as refreshing to an eye strained by too much sunlight as a slice of cucumber. Clotilde wasn't enamoured of our too-Tuscan look, however: the cactus-like state of those islands in the south was what really appealed to her.

As for food, this woman, beautiful even as she grew older, used to exclaim with delight when the *melanzane* (aubergines) and *koliokathaki* (courgettes) came to the table combined in Maria's delicious easy ratatouille. 'This is what I make on Sefiros,' she says – but in Clotilde's case one must envisage her going by mule or donkey down to the port at dawn to collect her food: her life is as austere and hard as ours is shamefully sybaritic. We hear of Clotilde in the hurricane winds of that sparsely populated, bare island, tying herself to a chair to paint. And we agree, when she has gone, that her dedication is worth it. Her paintings are unforgettable.

Chapter Nine

Late Summer

A description in Homer's *Odyssey* of the garden at King Alcinous' palace, thought to have been sited at Paleocastritsa, seems at first surreal with 'cluster on cluster' of grapes and 'fig upon fig' always coming to perfection, with 'some of the grapes drying in the sun, while on foremost rows hang unripe bunches that have just cast their blossom'. But it's a metaphor for the 'spring all the year round' for which Corfu is famed. 'Vegetable beds are neatly laid out beyond the farthest row and make a smiling patch of never-failing green' could exactly describe the allotments below Liapades where leeks, carrots, onions and artichokes can be counted on for most of the year. Wild broom's yellow flowers appear, like the snowdrops, before autumn is even done; and the misty-blue rosemary makes a winter show while late summer is still in full swing.

High summer blends almost imperceptibly into late summer; the end of August when the Lion turns to the Virgin, the season most loved by visitors for its sun, empty beaches, and of course its fruit. Even if there is a sea-fog – such as befell my mother when she was trying to row home up the coast and was caught in a curtain of invisibility similar to that imposed by Athene when disguising Odysseus – the sun nearly always disperses it by midday. And the recent violent storms around the September equinox seem little changed since the deluges which accompanied the Homeric hero's shipwreck off our bay.

We are at the long table, it's past two and the returning near-shipwreck victims clamber up the steps and long wild sage-and-rosemary-bordered path to the terrace. When they arrive, my daughter looks pale, as if the fog has washed her cheeks with white vapour, and my mother seems, to put it mildly, hugely relieved. But the sight of the meal we are waiting to eat with them brings colour and a stronger tone of voice all round, for here, to be eaten after the leg of lamb cooked with its blackened onions and bowl of steaming *kokinogouli* (the green vegetable with a red root), is the pudding we all like best when high summer shades into the fifth season of Corfu. Tiny seedless grapes lie on a bed of brown sugar and yoghurt. A separate dish at the side contains our own new crop of the scented strawberry grape that grows, dark as an embroidered tapestry, on a grid outside the sitting-room window that overlooks the sea. The bunches are plentiful and have been watched closely for signs of ripening – and at last here they are, along with a bunch of muscats from the vine at the back of the house. We feel as if we're in Alcinous' garden – and decide, when *carpouzi*, the bright red watermelon, is fetched from the cold store room behind the kitchen, that we'll save it for another day: the grapes make enough pure pleasure in themselves.

The recent stranding of the two rowboat passengers leads to arguments and half-memories of how that wily Greek did in fact come into Rovinia Bay; and in the end, along with strong coffee and more retsina, Homer's *Odyssey* is brought from its shelf. We read out the story of Odysseus' sea journey and perilous landing just below where we sit now.

For all that landscape, sea and setting seem unchanged since the days of Homer, things are different this year. It has rained when it has never in living memory done so, that is, before the Ascension of the Virgin Mary on August 15th, and so the extraordinary dustiness and dryness associated with the heavy, herby smell from the mountains and the brown, pine-cone-scattered ground, are overlaid with a faint haze of green. The rushing down of the torrent when there is no record of such a phenomenon at the zenith of late summer is like an earthquake in its unexpectedness and its intimations of a planet grumbling and exploding at intolerable pressures. We, humankind, have brought the fierce forest fires that now threaten us at Rovinia from as nearby as Lakones. We, foolish and vain, have released the chemicals which bring these disruptions to the natural cycle. But a self-invited visitor, revelling in the view of rushing water followed by a riverbed dried by the intense heat of the sun, sees it all without fearing for the future. And the fires don't worry her either: 'I've always thought it would be good to live by the sea,' she enthuses as a dark cloud, possibly smoke-filled, grows above the cliffs opposite. 'If the place catches alight, one can just run down to the beach!'

Thoughts of the imprudence of those who smoke and toss their cigarettes away into brush and scrub remind me of the little isthmus before it was touristified at Paleocastritsa: the pines, the scorched ground, the silence and the sea running up over sand. When we first came here in 1965 and stayed in the Tourist Pavilion, the one hotel with its small rooms and taverna, you could walk from one bay to the next without thinking of fire or of sudden squalls in the burning weeks before mid-August. Now, with everything uncertain, I can almost agree with our visitor that it's just as well to be able to rush, Gadarene-swine-like, to the beach below and leap into the sea.

Late summer, just as the swallows fly south from our verandah, brings a judge and his wife; and I see them in my mind's eye as swimmers who go right out to sea, slowly and methodically carving the gentle deep blue of an early September ocean into slices of pure azure. Humphrey, who is kind and thoughtful, brings us with a bump into the real world when, over our long, late summer meals under the strawberry vine, he tells of the terrifying crimes that have come before him in his travels from one city to the next, where he must pronounce sentence on wrongdoers. Pippa looks longingly at the wild cats which swarm up to the table when there's chicken or fish, and I feel grateful the swallows have gone so the cats can't stand in their long wait under the nests for the fledglings to fall into their mouths. Having run restaurants and clubs, Pippa knows so much about food that it's gratifying to Maria, and my mother too, to hear her enthusiastic comments.

Yet, for all the excellent dishes provided in that halcyon time before the autumn equinoctial storms, I think of these friends as surrounded by the dark grapes, hanging like Bacchus' crown just above our heads at the table, and carried round when the weather's still warm, but not so hot that you have to lurk indoors. This is a scene where wine, red or white at three or four pounds for a two-litre bottle, and grapes, often the many-pipped *carpouzi*, make a fresco of colour that demands and gets that painterly essential: a splash of red.

Late Summer Food

Food eaten in the dog days and beyond needs to be light – tempting to those who have been so long in the sea they taste salt on their lips as they lift fork or spoon for the first life-saving mouthful. The reviving spinach in Greece's most famous dish, *spanokopita*, is perfect, though late summer is a season that goes on a long time – from mid-July to the end of September – and all the following dishes are excellent when eaten at this time of year.

Spanakópita is the treat produced in Greece when a good friend or relative looks in – a fluffy spinach tart in filo pastry.

Spanakópita

1 packet filo pastry
2 lbs / 1 kg fresh spinach, finely chopped
1 onion, finely chopped
1 tin chopped tomatoes
1 wineglass olive oil
1 oz / 25 g feta cheese, crumbled
1 oz / 25 g Gouda cheese, grated
3-4 eggs, depending on their size
butter
salt and pepper to season

Heat the oil in a pan, and fry the onion until browning. Add the tomatoes and season with a little salt and pepper. Add the spinach and stir to wilt.

Remove the pan from the heat then crumble in the feta, add the Gouda and break in the eggs. Allow this spinach mixture to cool slightly and then mix the ingredients together well.

Butter an oven dish, spreading the dish with half the packet of filo pastry, then fill this pie case with the spinach mixture. Lid the pie with the remaining layers of pastry, one by one, each brushed with melted butter. Ensure that the edges of the filo case are pinched closed and that the spinach mixture inside does not show. Finish off the pastry top with a good brushing of more melted butter.

Bake in a preheated hot oven to start for about 10 minutes, then at a low heat for about half an hour. The pie is ready when steaming hot and golden.

Aubergine Salad

Serves 6

4 large aubergines
juice of 2 lemons
4 fl oz / 120 ml olive oil
1 clove garlic
¼ onion, chopped
olive oil to taste
salt

Roast the aubergines wrapped in foil, with a little oil rubbed over each one, in a medium-hot oven for about 1 ¼ hours until very soft. Cool the aubergines slightly and then scoop out flesh and purée in blender with the lemon juice, garlic, onion and a little salt. Add olive oil to taste. Serve cooled with plenty of crusty bread and green salad leaves.

A really local recipe, this translates as 'chicken cooked in the way of the village'.

Kotopoulo Xoriatikos

Serves 4–6

8 pieces of chicken, the skin left on
2 lbs / 1 kg potatoes, peeled and chopped
1 small wineglass fresh oregano (rigani), chopped
1 large wineglass olive oil
6 whole garlic cloves, peeled
juice of 2 lemons
salt and pepper to season

In a roasting pan, arrange the pieces of chicken, the garlic cloves and the potatoes, halved or quartered depending on their size. Season with salt, pepper and the oregano.

Pour over olive oil to completely cover the bottom of the pan, and drizzle also over the meat and potatoes.

Roast in a medium oven for 1¼ to 2 hours. Pierce the chicken with a skewer to ensure that the meat is cooked all the way through: the juices should run clear. When the dish is done, remove from the oven and add the lemon juice and ¼ mug of hot water, poured down the corner of the dish. Stir once and serve with bread to mop up the juices.

The classic Greek hors d'oeuvre.

Hummus

4 oz / 100 g chickpeas, soaked overnight and drained
juice of 2 lemons
3 tablespoons tahina paste
2 garlic cloves, crushed
salt to season

Simmer the chickpeas in fresh water for about 1 hour, then drain them, reserving the cooking liquid. In a blender, purée the chickpeas with lemon juice, tahina, garlic and salt, and enough of the cooking liquid to obtain a soft, creamy consistency.

To serve, garnish with a dribble of olive oil and a dusting of paprika.

Greek Tomato Salad

Serves 6

6 tomatoes
1 small wineglass fresh oregano (rigani), chopped
1 small wineglass fresh basil, chopped
1 onion, finely chopped
6 oz / 150 g feta cheese
1 large wineglass olive oil
salt and pepper to season

Slice the tomatoes across their width and salt them. Sprinkle amongst the slices the oregano, onion, feta and basil. Toss with cracked pepper and olive oil and leave to rest for 10—15 minutes before serving, so that the flavours mingle.

Pastitsia

Serves 6

macaroni, ribbon width
1 lb / 500 g minced beef
2 onions, chopped
small wineglass olive oil
small wineglass fresh basil, chopped
small wineglass bay leaves
1 teaspoon cinnamon
1 tin peeled tomatoes
2 heaped tablespoons tomato purée
1 wineglass water
béchamel sauce
salt and pepper to season

Cook the pasta in salted boiling water, stirring once or twice, for two minutes until al dente. Drain and set to one side. In a pan, heat the olive oil and fry the onions, basil, cinnamon and bay leaves and season with salt and pepper. When the onions have yellowed from the cinnamon and are beginning to brown, add the tomatoes, tomato purée and one wineglass of water. Do not overheat, but cook gently for 10 minutes, stirring occasionally. Now, transfer with the beef mince to another bowl and stir vigorously.

Butter a casserole dish. Make a béchamel sauce, making sure that it is not too thick.

Into the casserole dish pour in layers the macaroni, tomato and mince sauce, and béchamel. One layer of each should fill a large dish. Bake in a medium oven for half an hour or until thoroughly cooked.

Papallini are tiny fish and very good fried and squeezed with lemon juice.

Papallini

Wash and clean the fish and drain carefully. Place them in a plastic bag with salt and flour, and shake to coat the fish. Heat sweetcorn or sunflower oil until very hot and shallow fry the fish for about 10 minutes, turning once.

Serve with a jar of freshly squeezed lemon juice and olive oil.

Mezes are currently all the rage in London, and it seems the right time to talk about them here, right at the end of late summer before autumn and then winter sets in, and eating with our toes dabbling in the Ionian, or on a stone terrace at a friend's house on the other side of the island, becomes an impossibility.

The friend in question, provider of the most famous *mezes* in Corfu, is named Marily and she lives with her husband Neil McVicar, a retired Scottish judge, in Gastouri, a pretty, unspoilt village above Corfu Town. Marily is from an ancient Corfiot family, Voulgaris, which until the 1920s or so were owners of the body of St Spiridon, patron saint of the island. Whenever one meets Marily and hears stories about the saint it's tempting to imagine the refreshments often on offer – the tiny *dolmades*, little rolls of savoury rice in vine leaves; the purée of *melanzane*, aubergines peeled and pounded with garlic and oil; or the miniature *kephtedes*, rissoles of herb-infused minced lamb – sustaining Spiridon on his arduous journey from Cyprus to Corfu.

Marily's *mezes* are in great part her own invention, coupled with recipes handed down in the old house in Gastouri. We visit right at the end of October, when the season is changing and there is more emphasis on mouthfuls of hot heaven – tiny fish like whitebait; grilled *mesithra*, a crumbly white cheese; and portions of octopus – than on the olives, cucumber and hummus always included in summer *mezes*. And our journey back across the island shows us how far the autumn in this wonderful place likes to fake another spring: we stop by the side of the road and look at snowdrops under a bridge.

Autumn Journal 2002

September 9th

Returning to Rovinia when the season described by Hesiod as 'exhausting summer' is on the way out, nevertheless produces some surprises, not all of them pleasant.

We'd heard a week before leaving London that the torrent, the water which fills the dried-out riverbed that bisects our valley, had once again come rushing down to the sea. 'I don't know what anyone coming to view the place would make of it now,' I said when we clumped down the pebbled mosaic steps earlier today and the extent of damage caused by the torrent was revealed to us.

The beach, not to put too fine a point on it, looks as if it has been bitten and spat out, chewed remnants of titanic boulders and showers of sharp stones making it hard to attain the shore in several places. The sheer weight and speed of the rushing torrent has carved out banks of an ugly yellowish colour, against which a succession of abandoned rowing-boats and broken caiques lean drunkenly. 'Nausicaa wouldn't even have been able to get down here,' someone jokes, 'not with all that washing and a retinue of maidens anyway.'

My mother, as so often, restores the sense of balance needed in this distressing situation and reminds us that the last time the torrent came down, in early spring, it took another gigantic storm to restore the beach to beauty; soft, glistening sand dunes filling in the ravaged riverbed and the new estuary formed by the angry, scavenging cascade taken away overnight. 'The difference is,' she agrees, as Thodoros remarks that this has never happened before at this time of year, that we, like everyone else in the world, are having to learn to live in a fast-changing climate, violent and unpredictable. This is the week of the Johannesburg summit and the US has refused to back the Kyoto agreement. Standing in the moonscape created by the August torrent, I look up the bed of dry stones to the Judas tree and the grove, green as it has never been before at this time of year. All very beautiful; there are early cyclamens growing in what look like the ruins of an ancient city, so vast are the pillars and crumbling shapes created by the now-vanished river. But wrong: the coming down of the torrent in high summer has set everything at Rovinia askew. Tonight (it is late now and I have woken in blackness, the new moon having slipped over the hill opposite hours ago) I dream of a ruined house – ours, sitting atop an eroded cliff. I wander there awhile, then sleep.

September 11th

What better day than September 11th, when half the world mourns, arms for war, discusses and pontificates over the strange new empire we now inhabit, than to look at the plants and herbs which have grown here and have lasted through coups and gods, emperors and conquerors, acting as prophylactics and cures, as tastes and pleasures which go back to the beginning of recorded existence? Some we found when we came here: the wild fig and the olives and the thyme which grows high above us in the hills and provides that honey-musty smell unique to Greece. In ancient times, the herbs would have been gathered, some dried and hung as a bouquet to mark Corfu's perpetual spring. Rosemary, with its pale blue flowers that come out beside the sea even in the roughest of winter storms, would have been stuffed into lamb; *barbounia* (red mullet), plentiful in the Ionian, was best cooked on beds of wild fennel (*marathra*) – and which we pick two bays down to the south, along with *tsimbala* (samphire), and bring back in the little caique to the house. Would the dwellers in the antique world have savoured the bitter, dark green taste of samphire, first mentioned in literary terms nearly two and a half thousand years later in *King Lear*? Would the juice of a lemon and a dash of olive oil be considered then a suitable dressing to go with this subtle wild plant? Though the ancient Greeks didn't use basil in their cuisine, we grow it in pots at the back of the house, and, with its small, curly leaf disconcertingly unlike the large, quickly tiring leaves of the plant bought in London markets or greengrocers, made into Maria's pesto sauce, it's irresistible.

September 15th
Tim returns from one of his walks and tells of a meeting with the man who (pretty well single-handedly) built our new road. Now he's enthusing about the next project, it seems. 'It will be another new road,' Spiro the builder had waved energetically in the direction of the village of Liapades behind us, today enclosed in September mists. Tim enquired excitedly about the exact positioning of this new road. Will it cut across our land? We see ourselves for a moment as emulating the heroic Swampy of England's M1, clinging to his condemned tree for months as the diggers and dumpers come daily closer. Will the road run behind the two small houses belonging to two sisters, daughters of Dassia, a frequent visitor and friend of Maria and Thodoros? One of the sisters is married to someone high up in the Greek Government: if the motorway we already imagine wrecking our valley comes close behind their modest buildings (their land was somehow left out of the equation when pieces of the patchwork of olive grove and scrub on the hillside were bought all of forty years ago), will the sisters get a word in the ear of the relevant minister in Athens and ensure we are all left in peace?

The more we peer up the valley, past the ruined well with the fig tree and on up to the now-invisible terrace with the hexagonal tower (where friends once decided to crack the problem of the steep climb to their retreat by putting luggage or shopping in an electric wheelbarrow: it ran away with them and careered down the slope to end upside down in the grove), the more we realise what a good positioning for a coastal road, a glamorous *corniche*, this part of Rovinia's eleven acres would make. A word in an ear – essential in Greece and sometimes referred to as a 'p', a plea accompanied by a stiff bundle of notes, seems the only way forward. But we don't have access to an ear, here or in the capital of this maddening, wonderful country. It was hard enough – in fact, it took almost two decades – to obtain permission for a road down to our own house. The then Mayor, a Melina Mercouri lookalike, while disappearing regularly into her own magic mist when approached by our excellent lawyer and by Thodoros and Thodoros' cousin Spiro the builder and asked to give a decision, was the one who in the end allowed access to Rovinia. The agreement depended on our supplying an area as a car park for tourists wishing to visit the beach, and this was gladly done. The road is also denoted as a Fire Road in the dangerously hot forest-fire summers which rage all over the island. However important, and indeed vital, to a continuation of life at Rovinia, our road is obviously minor compared with the construction on which Spiro is about to embark. Its progress will be beyond local control if it is to serve the western coast of the island. We await reports from Tim's next walk when he will hope to find Spiro on the site of the projected road – but no further news ever comes. Like so many Greek dramas, the projected motorway vanishes into thin air.

CORFU BANQUET

September 20th

Breakfast when we arrived could be had on the terrace, but today is dark and threatens more of the rain which has brought such a bushiness to the forest on the hill across the valley and carpeted the grove both sides of the riverbed in an unnatural bright green. I go out to look down at a flat sea and sigh over a lost summer, only last week, when the blue table outside was laden with strawberry grapes from the big vine beyond the long sitting room, and Maria's *avgho-bacon* – fried egg with delicious crispy little squares of bacon and toasted bread – sat next to the old brown teapot. Will that Greek summer weather ever come back again? Will I eat Maria's dark, scrumptious marmalade made from Rovinia oranges in the strong rays of the sun before autumn takes a real hold and nets to catch the olives are spread out under the trees?

As so often before, this turns out to be an unnecessary question. By the time we've gone down to a warm sea (whatever the weather, it's impossible not to) the sun has burned away the mist, magic or otherwise, and all the little boats coming across from Paleocastritsa are clearly visible to us. There's no sign, either, that the predicted storms will do anything other than what they usually do, which is to gather and concentrate on the heights of the village of Lakones, high on the volcanic mountain that towers above our bay. Already, an indigo battle has begun up there; but we swim, and then drink a glass of ouzo with feta and tiny, black Corfiot olives on a terrace blazing with a new *megalo kalokairi* (high summer) sun.

September 23rd

I was completely wrong about the weather. One glance at the glass in the hall would have shown a plummeting needle. Sinisterly rising temperatures over the past two days have meant going to bed with the outdoor thermometer registering close on 26 °C / 80 °F, and long, sticky nights where even a sheet is too heavy to bear. We've passed the equinox, and these are doubtless the storms which accompany times of equal lengths of hours of darkness and light; but, due to all the anxiety over global warming which fills the papers just now, nothing feels very equal. My aunt, visiting for the first time in two years, tells a tale of a girl sitting by a cottage fireplace in Ireland, struck by lightning which comes down the chimney and seeks her out. I'm tempted to wear rubber-soled shoes even indoors: the flashes of venomous electricity, immediately followed by bangs of aptly-named Greek *donda*, are enough to make one believe in the possibility of angry gods high up in the mountains circling the Plain of Ropa and the sea.

Although the lights have twice briefly gone out, it's comforting to go into the kitchen and see the preparations for *sofrito*, that Corfiot speciality with a dark, glistening sauce. Maria is particularly preoccupied; a friend from the *poli*, Corfu Town, and his wife, she an expert who has been on TV with her recipe for the preparation of *sofrito*, are coming to lunch tomorrow. In case we're without power for an indefinite time, it's safest to make the dish today. Afterwards, we'll have the *pagota fragole*, the wild strawberry ice cream made by Maria in May, when punnets of the delicious scented *fraise du bois* were on sale all over the town. The Venetian architecture of Corfu, the washed pinks and reds of the tall, elegant houses seem to belong with the taste of these woody, subtle fruit. When the French took over in 1798 and built their little Rue de Rivoli there, the Liston, it added a sense of excitement and enjoyment with its ice cream and pâtisserie shops. After the wild strawberries come apricots and melons from stalls in the market and outside the greengrocers huddled in narrow streets, and Maria makes her ice cream, to be eaten right through the summer and the autumn months. Tomorrow, when (and if, given the forecast of dreadful storms) our little lunch party takes place, we'll be transported by the taste of the berries to the pure, blue days of May. But Maria is too busy perfecting the *sofrito* for which she is justly well known in these parts to consider the vagaries of the weather. Now there's a road to the house, her expression says when I express my doubts, people can come here storm or shine. But the steep pebble steps down to the house, as I know, could deter the townswoman in her high heels, and the crowding olives by the path can be liable to succumb to a lightning strike. '*Dhen pirazei,*' Maria mutters as she stirs the sauce which comes from another of her secret recipes. 'It doesn't matter. It will be all right.'

September 24th
The storm – lightning, thunder and a high wind – came last night. None of us slept as the house shook and rattled in its grip. But now it's almost over, leaving a lake on the

terrace and a spreading stain on the tiles in the sitting room by the French windows.

While we wait for the storm to blow itself out, I go to the edge of the terrace and look down at what we all hope will be a changed and restored landscape. For the sheer weight of the waves which pound in can cover over the ravages caused by the torrent. Our beach will be a brochure dream again, with new sand and only the old beach chairs providing an eyesore. What if the angry sea swallowed them too, I can't help cruelly thinking; then we'd be as pristine a bay as when Odysseus scrambled in here, in a storm identical to the one we're suffering now.

Of course I know there's no chance of anyone from Rovinia being able to go down and remove the rusting beach-chair-cum-mattresses piled so blatantly in the middle of the beach. Along with the abandoned pedaloes at the entrance to the grove just past high-water mark, the chairs give an uncared-for aspect to the bay. But who owns these unseaworthy craft is hardly known by now: what is certain is that their removal or dumping up where the rubbish is collected in our new car park would bring the owner as quickly from the bushes as the sight of a princess and her maidens flushed out a shipwrecked sailor. Just as it's true that you're never alone in Greece, so also is it true that every inch of rotting scrap metal has its owner just waiting to pounce and sue.

The storm has almost passed and I begin a slippery descent to the beach, holding on to bushes of wild rosemary as I go. For I'm looking for traces of the surprising arrival of a little boat the night before the storm got underway, which came in to our jetty at ten o'clock, a red lamp burning brightly in its prow. The cave lights were on, so the incomers could hardly have been smugglers. As it's been put about by wags in the village that Rovinia possesses, James Bond movie-like, its own nuclear bomb buried here at the edge of the bay, we joked that the cops have come at last, to unveil our evil activities. But through binoculars, Tim reported that an immensely tall black man (we've seen him by day on the beach and have speculated as to which country he reigns over) had stepped from the small boat with a red lamp and changed into a rubber wetsuit. A companion, Greek presumably, joined him. 'What on earth were they doing?' I asked Maria the next morning, and was rewarded by a grumpy face. For she had heard, as I had, the boat's engine when it finally left.

'Three in the morning,' Maria says, adding casually that they must have been hunting down an octopus. We'd both been woken, and perhaps the implication was that we should have been offered some of the delicacy for our broken night. Well, better than a nuclear bomb, I thought; but I'm still mystified, as so often, by the comings and goings in Rovinia Bay.

With such thoughts, a stormy day on the west coast of this complicated and lovely island is whiled away. Mysteries abound; but so do delicious meals and inspired new stories from Maria. I quote to her the song I heard when I first visited Corfu in the 1960s, a folk song for a wedding, which the white-haired sister of Marie Aspioti, our late and much-

loved Corfiot teacher and friend, recited to me one evening
of dancing and festivities organised for the journalists'
group I was in. '*Mirizei, mirizei, octopodi kai risi!*' 'There's a
smell of octopus and rice!' goes the song, and Maria,
although staunchly denying that any such words are ever
put to music at the time of nuptials, agreed that octopus, if
prepared to her specifications, could provide a feast for
any special occasion.

Octopodi

*The octopus is killed by hurling it against a rock — this also makes it
tender to eat.*

*Build a fire on the beach, cover slices of the octopus with salt and
chopped rigani, and place on a grill, fairly high above the flames. When
the slices blacken, turn them over.*

Eat hot, sitting cross-legged on the sand, with cold salamura sauce.

The Nikterida (meaning bat, a word we come to dread shortly, when approaching winter appears to be presaged by a shoal of night-flyers, inky black against the moonlit sea) is the name of the taverna we love to visit whenever possible, up on the steep road into Liapades.

Even if the vine over the small terrace right on the road has an irritating habit of dying off just over one's head (and today a piece of bamboo has been placed over the hole), there are few places more congenial than Yorgos and family's restaurant. You're bang in the middle of village life – the van, the motorbikes, the robust old woman on the donkey and the crippled granny with her stick – and the playground of the school lies right beneath, a drop down from Yorgos' new DIY store, installed under the taverna. The noise is frequently so loud that you can't hear what anyone is saying. The few tourists who drop by seem stunned at first; but they soon succumb, as we know we will, to the friendliness of Yorgos and his son Costa, the delicately shredded salad *xoriatiki*, the excellent *calamari* in batter, and lamb on a spit.

September 25th

After the brief respite yesterday, the storm resumed with terrifying intensity. Tim – trapped in the little guest house along the pebbled cliff path, unsafe to walk on in thunderstorms when lightning flashes yellow as spikes of gorse or broom on the tangle of wild vegetation beside it – later describes the experience as resembling a trip over Niagara in a tin bucket. The bangs and drum rolls that come in from the west settled for a huge dispute right over the roof of the main house which, with its lightning conductor, gives protection to the tiny building. This is now hidden from sight by a wall of pounding rain, a wild display of dancing and writhing by the olive tree now grown to a good height at the top of the steps down to the beach, and an afternoon darkness which is reminiscent of the eclipse of the sun a year back, when we cowered in a Dorset garden to witness it. 'Perhaps it's the end of the world,' we say, peering out through misted windows at the invisible path to the small house. 'He can't have decided to go out for a walk, can he?'

Anxiety on this occasion was made much worse by the departure of my aunt for the airport. As soon as she had gone, it was clear that planes would not be able to come or go out of the island in a tempest such as this; and the disastrous aspect of my aunt's possible return to Rovinia, defeated until the storm ended in her aim to get home to London, was that the netting hammered over her window only the day before meant that closing the shutters in the bedroom she had occupied was now impossible. The notion had been mine: woken several nights running by rushing, slamming noises and cries of distress from her room down the corridor – a room which faces full frontal out to sea and bears the brunt of the squall (or typhoon if one such happens to be in the area) and violent winds and rain – I discovered each morning that bats, giant moths and the like had been rushing in through the open window. As the strawberry grape vine lies directly beneath, there was a good chance too of snakes, reputedly fond of curling up on top of the vine trellis, deciding to climb up into my aunt's room. Already she had received two hornets, which feasted on the grapes by day and liked to curl up in her curtains by night. Thodoros had fixed up the netting in ten minutes flat and we'd all felt relief that my aunt would no longer be prey to night horrors, as depicted by Goya or Hieronymous Bosch, in her stay by the seaside in Greece. Now, however, the snag in fixing the netting had become all too evident. The shutters could no longer be reached, and rain had poured in on to my aunt's bed, by the time we thought of groping our way upstairs in the afternoon blackness to look. We found ourselves hoping for the most undesirable of situations; one in which a plane takes off when it has no chance of gauging where the end of the runway may be, and when a squall as fierce as the ones we were suffering may lift even a Boeing right off the ground and into an adjacent lagoon.

'A bed in my room can be taken in there,' says my mother as the sopping mattress is dragged onto the floor and we stare at the netting as if the idea of putting it there has declared itself to be the work of someone either evil or stupid, in both cases certainly myself. 'And the bed frame,' she adds bravely, 'can be propped up on the landing.'

In the event, my aunt's flight to London took off four hours late and we saw the 767 to Gatwick twinkling thousands of feet above our bay before it went off into clear blue skies over Calabria. But the character of the storm had been so powerful that it stayed with us, like the disruptive creatures we had now shut out, all night. It was a reminder of the Greek ability of a minor event (a caller from London showed no excitement when I tried to describe the drama of the lightning and ear-splitting thunder) to disrupt as fully as the occupants of my poor aunt's waking nightmares. 'A *catastrophe*,' says Maria, when she sees the water spreading in under the windows and settling under the table at the end of the room where we eat. At first it seems she is the only one to get our storm in proportion. But then it's pointed out that catastrophe, in Greek, means merely flood.

September 26th

Belinda, a friend from London, comes to call and tells us of her life in Tuscany. A recent book, *Under the Tuscan Sun*, has brought unwelcome sightseers to her area near Cortona, and we all fall silent, wondering what would happen in the unlikely event of tour buses bumping down the new road to the parking space at the top of our steps. Would people insist on seeing round? How could we cope with the influx? But it does seem unlikely, we all agree: this isn't Tuscany, the new road is very hard to find, and those few who express an interest in Rovinia usually do so because they're whiling away their time on the beach. Once the taxi-boat comes to collect them, they vanish into an unlimited expanse of sea, cliff and yet more sea.

We're told of a new restaurant by our visitor, and we realise how, as so often, strangers know far more than we do about the island's growing amenities. 'Nakos,' Belinda says, 'is right in the Shell garage on the Plain of Ropa road. But don't be put off. It's excellent.'

And so it turns out to be: a small, pleasant room with a log fire and the best and most interesting food we've had in a taverna for years.

In what seems another age, before the rains and angry skies, we sat at the long table on our verandah and enjoyed a meal that was pure summer, light and subtle-tasting. Swordfish with a lemon and oil *salamura* sauce and its accompaniments were as delightful to look at as to eat. But, as so often seems to be the case in this idyllic place, stories of breakdown, rescue and Greek generosity lie behind the meal – and I, staying behind that morning to work in my room, was the only one unaware of the perils involved in producing it.

The first sign that something had gone amiss I mistook for another of those coincidences or 'combinations' as my mother and I term them, which dog all arrivals and departures at Rovinia, particularly by sea. Sitting on the terrace after a morning's work, and only slowly realising that it's close on one-thirty and thus late for the return of the party that went down the coast in the *Faleina* (my mother, my aunt Anne, and Tim, with Thodoros at the helm with the intention of pulling a fish from the Ionian while the others swim in a promising cove), I see a large tourist caique make its way noisily up to our jetty, the *Faleina* close behind. 'Typical,' I think, wondering at the lack of good manners displayed by the caique's captain and deciding, foolishly, that he must be non-Greek: a foreign rep, probably, training in the art of navigating our waters on the west coast of the island. 'He might have let our boat in,' I mutter. 'After all, we built the pier and it's the entrance to Rovinia. Why do the tourists always have precedence over the inhabitants here?'

Almost everything turned out to be a mistake in my perception of events, as I was soon to understand. For one thing, the big caique, which if I had been correct in my assumptions would have been jam-packed with people, blaring music and all, was as empty and deserted as a ghost ship. I thought for a moment of the dreadful vessel in Werner Herzog's *Nosferatu* as it comes noiselessly into Amsterdam, only the devil's cargo of plague-infested rats aboard. The cutting out of the engine made the unexpected arrival all the more spooky – and, come to think of it, the wind had to be in the south to make Rovinia Bay the only place safe to dock, for these large boats. Today, white ribbons of foam are trying their hardest to become horses against the cliffs by the way in to Paleocastritsa, just below the monkey's head. In fact, you would say the monkey was wearing little more than a lacy bib. So what is this caique doing here at all?

The uncharitable thought that Rovinia may have become a destination whatever the weather, thus fulfilling my late father's worst expectations of constant 'pop', reggae, Garage or whatever the Club Med or Club Corfu likes to produce in tourist-infested Cavos in the south of the island, is soon banished by a few moments of intense worry on the whereabouts of our own little caique, containing Thodoros and the family party. It's as if they've been swallowed by the large, empty fishing-vessel, and have indeed become like Jonah and the whale. Thodoros had been trying to come in to the jetty, had been beaten to it by the phantom navigator of the deserted big caique, and now had disappeared, along with my mother, my aunt and Tim, altogether. For one further dreadful minute I wondered if this passengerless – and possibly rudderless – craft filling up the placid waters near the cave, was in fact a hallucination: a simulacrum of the old caique we'd had when my father was alive. Was it an apparition, a warning of a fatal accident on my mother's first outing of the season, down the coast?

The truth lay in the fact of this being a maiden journey for the little *Faleina*, or at least since the season of summer visitors. But the engine had been newly serviced – what could have gone wrong?

No sooner had Thodoros dropped the family on an empty beach at Iliodorus than the engine had conked out. Rather, the usual gods of combinations saw to it that he'd chuntered way out of sight and had put down a line to fish when the engine went. And of course the happy swimmers, exclaiming at the clarity of the water and the cliffs sprouting with all the wild herbs they wanted, to be picked after swimming and brought back for cooking with the fish Thodoros would most certainly catch, these swimmers had no inkling of the fate which had befallen Thodoros.

Nor did they know – so that same god would have whispered it in their ear before long – that Thodoros' mobile phone had gone as dead as the caique engine some days back, and a new battery was promised in the town. He couldn't, as now required by law, ring the harbour at Paleocastritsa for help. The swimmers received no telepathically transmitted picture of the stranded *Faleina* – at least not until the appointed time to be picked up had passed. Then a good many pictures must have crowded in.

So what I saw below me in the bay was a tourist caique with a generous and good-hearted captain, who, having spotted Thodoros' well-known small blue and white caique drifting, had offered to tow them all the way back to Rovinia.

Here they are, my aunt having darted up the ladder on the side of the empty tourist caique and dancing like a girl on deck while visitors to the beach look on in surprise at this odd arrival. By the time the whole party has climbed the steps and path to the house, the episode has already become one of the closed chapters of this place: everyone is safe; the wind is in fact in the process of changing to the south and so, as if to exact a toll for the near-accident, the Captain will bring his September load of hotel folk to the beach and there will be music and wine and the black smoke from the barbecue that goes up outside the cove, where they build it on the damp sand.

This time, however, there must be a good drink for the friend who pulled in our little boat: he'll come and sit on the edge of the balustrade and knock back the Botrys brandy that has stayed in the sitting room cupboard since my father died. And we'll talk of the time the distinguished general came to lunch all those years ago – General Spiers was his name – and how he missed his footing when taking his leave from the newly constructed jetty, so that he fell right in the sea. Arrivals and departures are difficult, here, we agree: you can't tell which combination will come for you. But one of the most common, we do concur, is a major storm or wind-change when at sea, which means rushing in the small caique to the safety of the bay at Alipa – when the car had been left right across a stormy expanse at the harbour in Paleocastritsa.

October 1st

Autumn comes in swathes of cyclamen, pink and pale red Turkish Delight rosewater colours, heliotrope and scarlet and a vivid purple. They clamber on the old walls down the garden, and self-seeded pink lilies grow tall amongst them; they lie in sheets of lilac and mauve under the olives and are tall and stately themselves this year, thanks to all the rain that fell in August. 'They're like cyclamens in a shop,' my mother says as the dark silver-striped leaves unfurl around the blooms; and it's true they make me think of the flower stand on the corner at home in London, where an array of bright cyclamens in pots marks autumn's coming in.

I'll have to go soon, but I'm determined not to miss this new season in Corfu, with all its repeated and suddenly remembered moments, conversations, and its alternating heat and cool. 'We'll make sure the rotting timbers of the old boats no one wants will be cleared away before the winter storms come right up past the high-water mark and make it hard to get at them,' we promise ourselves.

Someone points out that prospective buyers may be put off by the sea-junkyard that appears to grow out of the beach. If they are though, the rest of us reply robustly, then the rare peace and beauty of Rovinia should not be theirs.

October 5th

With only occasional memories of late summer – spattered and blown to bits by the storms we've suffered, it's true, but returning always to the Greek-sun-and-sea look which draws visitors to Corfu, and rightly so – we're now in autumn indeed, with more than just cyclamens and drowsy wasps to show it.

We're walking down the grove on an October day, my mother and I, and she sees the first yellow and white flash under an olive tree, calling out so urgently that I think she must have caught sight of a fox or a rabbit.

Fox, in fact, is how the chanterelle is known – or was so in my childhood in Scotland, when these highly coloured fungi could be found under beech trees.

Here, where the olives display at their roots an abundance of flowers all year round – marigold, mallow, dandelion – it comes as a surprise each year to find the much paler wild mushroom; and before long we hold a small bunch of the scented treasures. Do they smell of fox? Perhaps, but autumn brings the stink to wood and dell – even as far down as the marine landscape that, in summer, we see and believe we live in to the exclusion of all else. We go triumphantly up to the house and into the kitchen, where we spread our booty on the kitchen table. Maria gives a secret smile, lifts them perfunctorily, and disappears down into the grove.

It's dark and we've made an olive-wood fire for the first time since the cold spring that already seems to be so long ago. The evenings are drawing in, and bundles of twigs tied in cones like witches' hats lie piled in the log cupboard by the living-room window. To go there and collect from the shelves fuel stored still with some of the summer warmth, is to walk under the strawberry vine, huge and dark and still festooned with bunches of ruby grapes; and a walk in the galloping twilight is something of an adventure. The myths don't escape one, even in so domestic a task; and a bat, preparing itself doubtless for its nightly visit to my aunt's window above the trellis, swoops low and almost brushes my cheek, bringing back memories of Homer's description of the Underworld. There, bats twitter and chirp, and are the souls of the dead. Here, I remind myself as I dump a pile of lichen-covered logs on the shelf outside the living-room door, we live in the modern world. I'll go and pick a sprig of the last of the mint from the pot outside the kitchen: it'll bring a summery taste to our drink, sipped this time from the side of a delightful fire and not on the terrace facing a cooling, wind-whipped sea.

But even here, the mint leaves have shrunk on their branches and I'm reminded that it was because Pluto, King of the Underworld, had fallen in love with a beautiful young woman, that his wife Persephone had insisted on the transformation of her rival into a lowly plant. To make amends, the gods made the poor young woman smell as good as the invention of a new scent, mint, could make her. Yet today, sorting out the leaves from their withered siblings, I realise the season of this summer treat is over. Summer is over. Autumn has finally and definitively come.

All of this is made up for at supper. Maria has been talking about her childhood and family and we have been listening avidly, my mother translating those parts I can't understand. As she speaks, and as we look across the fire at her, we see she holds a bag – two carrier bags in fact – and that she's about to spill the contents onto the table. 'Careful, Maria,' my mother warns as a soft bouquet of chanterelles descends onto our flimsy table. 'How could you have found so many? Careful, or they'll fall right off onto the floor.'

It had been Maria's finest hour and her secret smile is replaced with a beam of triumph. 'With both hands!' – she spreads her hands wide and bends, showing the extraordinary abundance produced by the earth – or so her almost mythological stance suggests. Under the roots of the olives, the little orange trumpets (much more highly coloured than the pale specimens we had found earlier) had risen to greet their natural plucker. And now we talk of the best way to cook these miraculous forest gifts: with pasta? As a risotto? Plain, on toast?

While Maria re-bags her catch of chanterelles and we sit down at the table with her, we hear her tales of her early years. And I jot them down, hoping for more tomorrow.

This is Maria's story.

Maria Repoulios was born in Liapades, the village above what was then the inaccessible and untouched Liapades (now Rovinia) Bay. 'We had enough to eat,' Maria says, 'because there was land up on the hill behind the village where we had olives and vines, and in the allotments we grew plenty of vegetables. My mother liked beans – and when I came down to the house built at Rovinia I cooked only village dishes – but in the War years and for a time after, very seldom we'd have meat: lamb at Easter and Christmas and on some feast days, and we'd boil the old hens and find a way of making them tasty. That's why *kotopoulo xoriatikos* has become such a favourite – we knew how to make an old hen taste good. And if we didn't cook them in that way, it might be with macaroni and potatoes, tomatoes and onions.

'But on Sundays we had salt cod. And often, all week long, we'd have only *horta* (wild greens) and *fakes* (lentils) to eat after rising at daybreak and working all day.

'Five children slept in the family bed with *ya-ya* (grandmother) until they were fourteen or fifteen years old. Our family – I was the eldest child – consisted of two sisters and a brother, and a twin sister and brother who were carried about in a small basket. We were all in one room, the parents at one end and the children at the other. A long table, a bench, and a fire that smoked horribly because there was no chimney. The only one to have a room to himself was *papous* (grandfather).

'There was, of course, no light – just oil lamps and a big wooden sink for all the washing. And outside, at the back, was a row of five toilets for our street's houses.

'We had sweetcorn and garlic and lentils and green beans, but whatever appeared, grandfather wouldn't eat it, and he'd push the food in the fire. My father made us children wait for our bread so that grandfather could have some, and it was taken to him in his room. Father would bring in half a kilo of bread and say to him, "I'll kill you if you give this to the children."'

But the children didn't suffer. There were plenty of eggs, beans and *horta*, and Maria, sent each day to find the eggs, would quickly pierce a hole in one or two and drain the yolk on the way back home.

'Why are the hens laying so badly?' Maria's mother asked when these eggs were sucked. But Maria, who would also milk the three cows belonging to the family, drank from their udders too, and grew tall and robust.

Maria's mother liked to sing while she was sewing, and her children joined in. A peaceful scene, though one night, when Maria's father was out in the village, a woman who lived a short distance away came down through the pitch blackness with her oil lamp to ask permission for her son to marry Maria's sister Anna. Maria's father returned at just this point, over the potholed village road; and he was so surprised to see the woman standing there outside his house, lamp in hand, that he fell down a hole.

'My father was a good cook. He always did the meat, when we could have it, with a good sauce, and always put in cinnamon and paprika. Black pepper was a great luxury until after the War.'

When the Germans and the Italians were on the island, most of the girls in the village didn't dare go out and work in the fields: there were many rapes and scandals. And after bombs fell on Skripero, Maria's parents took her and the other children then born up to a cave in the hills. Maria's grandmother and aunt came too, and they all hid under the trees. When Maria crawled from her hiding-place to look at a German plane in the sky, her grandmother gave her a great slap across the face. Then Angeliki, the twin girl, fell out of her basket and had to be placed with her brother in a barrel, but the woman owner of the land refused the family permission to shelter in the cave. Maria's mother, who had a donkey with saddle-bags, gave the *andartes* (Resistance fighters) a billy-can of beans, but the enemy was near and she dropped the can and ran down into the riverbed to hide … these were some of the stories Maria told, on that autumn night. And here is the *fassolakia*, the bean stew, her mother cooked in Maria's childhood. *Fassolakia* kept Maria's family – and many others – from starvation in wartime and times of hardship: the beans, potato and onion make for a satisfying meal.

Fassolakia

Serves 4

2 lbs / 1 kg green beans
2 lbs / 1 kg potatoes
1 onion, chopped
large wineglass olive oil
salt and pepper to season

Wash, top and tail the green beans. Peel and slice the potatoes, not too thinly. In a large saucepan of boiling water, cook the beans and potatoes for 10 minutes, then discard half of the water so that the level reaches below the beans. Add the onion and the oil and season. Stir once and cook for a further 20 minutes. After this time, when the vegetables are tender, shake the pan once only, and serve.

Maria's Wedding

When Maria Repoulios married Thodoros Mazis on November 10th 1963, she and her fiancé had been engaged for two years, as was and remains the custom. Both from Liapades, they were considered the handsomest pair in the village: Maria a natural leader at dances and festivities, high-spirited and always ready for a joke; and Thodoros, well-dressed but unassuming with a quiet nature that suited him well to the life of a fisherman, the main way of life known to coastal village dwellers on the island.

That they had plans other than fulfilling the traditional roles became clear when Pandelios, the estate agent, reported to my parents shortly after the building of the house began, that 'a suitable couple' had approached him, saying they would like to find work with the foreigners who were making a new house down at Rovinia. Pandelios had engineered the sale of the land to my mother and father; and in the years which followed the seemingly endless negotiations over each strip and pocket of olive and vine, they had become firm friends.

But the recommendation of the trustworthy Pandelios turned out not to be necessary at all. It was clear from the start that this young couple – who had no inkling, naturally, of what to expect from the *xenoi* in the valley – were destined to get on exceedingly well at Rovinia. Maria's sense of humour and her desire to cook (she had only known the village dishes of her mother's house in Liapades) made every day an adventure. Soon she was to become an irreplaceable part of the house and life there. Thodoros, with his practical abilities – and his love of going out on the sea in a boat has never left him – also evolved into a good and trusted friend. Their house, down a vine-covered cobbled walkway at the back of Rovinia, has sylvan surroundings: arbutus, orange, lemon, olive and cypress trees grow on the land that slopes steeply down to the grove. The village house and land belonging to Thodoros and Maria Mazis was also retained by them, and they have two sons, Spiro and Nicos. Little Spiro and his younger brother Alexandros are the children of Nicos, manager of the Paradise restaurants in Paleocastritsa and near Skripero. Spiro also has a son, Thodoraki, and a daughter, Vasso.

So, family life from the start became an important feature of existence at Rovinia. Maria likes to remember her wedding day in Liapades which began it all; and she comes to perch on the balustrade at the edge of the terrace, the yucca trees planted so long ago now rising with their white plumes to form a feathery backdrop as she sits and talks.

Maria and Thodoros' engagement was unusual in that the bride-to-be and her intended husband stayed in her family home throughout the two-year period. It's normally the other way around, with the fiancée living under the thumb of a future mother-in-law for the duration, often being ordered about and in some cases maltreated, and possibly leading to a cancellation of the wedding.

'No, we all slept in one big room at home,' Maria says. 'My mother and father together, and myself with my sisters

Anna and Angeliki. No, we couldn't sleep together, my fiancé and I – although my brother's wife suggested this at one point. "If you do, I'll take a stick and beat everyone in sight," my mother said, so no one dreamt of suggesting it after that.'

I ask Maria if these customs still obtain in the village, and she answers of course not, that this was all of forty years ago. The need for a two-year waiting time was financial: to pay for a lavish wedding and provide the house linen, clothes and so on. A house appeared to have come bottom of the list as young couples stayed at home with parents and were often financially dependent on them. But everyone was poor, and it took all that time to prepare for the big day. By the sounds of it, the engagement party was as important an occasion as the wedding party itself.

'Thodoros' family gave jewellery – rings and watches – and house linen, and this started at eleven in the morning of the engagement party,' Maria says. 'They came down to my father's house and were served with *mezes*, liqueurs, ouzo and sweetmeats. Then we all went up to Thodoros' father's house with a band of accordion players following us. My family also gave dresses and shirts to Thodoros' family. Both of our mothers wore peasant dresses – those had a dark skirt with unpressed pleats and on top a white smocked shirt with wide sleeves and a little velvet waistcoat. Did you know that the head-dresses from each village were different, and that that was how you could tell where a woman came from? But in our case, all were from Liapades. Ours was made from plaiting a skein of thick white knitting cotton and twining it round the head above a folded cloth. Some villages have only a small blue-and-white checked gingham handkerchief as a head-dress.

'There were more refreshments up at Thodoros' family's house and we all danced in a neighbour's garden – joined from time to time by a four-month-old calf, which was quartered there. When we'd danced ourselves really hungry, we went back to my home for a large meal.'

As for the wedding itself, Maria tells us there was an even longer and more strenuous succession of feastings, dancings – and praying, in a service that lasted nearly two hours. The church in the *plateia* was full of men who walked and shouted amongst the worshippers, and children who gaped at her beautiful wedding dress and wreath of flowers.

'A dresser came to our house at 8 a.m.,' Maria remembers, and there was a great exchange of visits between families, with sweets and feta in abundance. 'A band came down to our house and the village girls came too, to help carry the trousseau up to Thodoros' house. Thodoros came down to our house too, while the bedroom was prepared for later. There were two mattresses, one of wool and one of cotton, which I provided. And,' adds Maria, laughing, 'the room was decked with red ribbons and the bedspread covered with presents of money, rice and sugared almonds. The girls had placed walnuts under the sheet, so that we wouldn't be able to sleep and would be forced to make love all night.'

As Maria describes the procession up to the church – her father and brother standing outside and holding red handkerchiefs, Thodoros waiting alongside for the appearance of his bride – the sun sets fittingly behind the monkey's head across the bay in a mass of scarlet streamers. Maria's words accompany us as we walk along the suddenly-dark terrace and we can hear the ghostly sound of the band playing in the *plateia* on Maria's wedding night, and smell the food that relatives and friends have been cooking at Thodoros' family's house since dawn. As we go back indoors, Maria is persuaded to reel off the succession of dishes enjoyed on that November day all those years ago. Proof that generosity and large appetites were as widespread then as now, the menu takes some beating – and it seems best to set it down here as it was presented. Little wonder that Maria recalls every detail to this day.

Maria's Corfu Banquet

According to Maria, 200 guests attended her wedding feast. The two families together produced 80 gallons of wine.

to start:
mezes — salami, cheese, ouzo and cognac

to follow:
mouscari, a beef and vegetable soup with macaroni

for main courses there were:
three whole sheep roasted in the village bread oven, cooked with potatoes, garlic, rigani and limoni and served with a huge plate of salad xoriatiki — the 'village salad' which mixes shreds of lettuce, cucumber, tomato, diced carrot — and a large piece of feta cheese

for the puddings:
a large tourta: a large open tart filled with cream, chocolate and vanilla, and on the table were grapes, apples and oranges. The mezes stayed on the table throughout the meal

and finally:
bonbonniera, a basket of sweets

Chapter Ten

Autumn Banquet

News of local elections make for much excitement – and this I hear about when back in London, and dreaming still of the chanterelles we had finally, with rice, on the evening when autumn declared itself in the first week of October. 'Yellow chamois leather,' I decide, and then feel this is too fanciful a description for the heavenly fungi. Yet the image of the fluted trumpets and the memory of their sharp, woody smell linger with me as my mother says with some triumph that a soup has now been concocted from the subterranean treasures. 'And there's a lot of celebrating going on,' she adds as I ask her to remind me of the way apples are done when placed on a slice of Corfiot orange and baked with brown sugar. 'A cousin,' – she means of Thodoros, I think – 'has become Mayor. There's a banquet tonight: no one expects to be home before five in the morning.'

AUTUMN BANQUET

'Where will the banquet be held?' I ask, remembering the sheer enormity of helpings and endlessly progressing courses at weddings and christenings and the like. 'Will it be a big event?'

'Oh, huge,' my mother says. 'It's in a restaurant on the road from Paleocastritsa up to Lakones. A real celebration, with at least two hundred people.'

The banquets I have heard described – or have on occasion been privileged to attend – are wonderful indeed, but it's impossible not to feel there's too much food, too expected a progression of roasts and super-sweet pastry tarts. But equally delicious, I can't help thinking, are the meals we have at home: the stuffed peppers and *stifado*, whether of rabbit or pork; the leg of lamb or shoulder, cunningly roasted with a little water and surrounded by the sweet local onions. And when people come to stay and *sofrito* makes its magnificent appearance, doesn't a meal outside at the long table with the sun dancing behind the pillars, or indoors at the table near the olive-wood fire, feel like a banquet for all the senses?

'And now winter does seem to be on the way,' my mother says. 'The last direct flight went back yesterday. And all the nets are down.'

Simple words, but the picture comes as sharp and vivid as if I had time-travelled to the west coast of the island to find myself walking – before the road from the village to the house was made – through groves suddenly black with nets to catch the small Corfiot olive as it drops from the tree. I pick my way carefully, and I smell the wood smoke of numberless bonfires as land is cleared before the coming winter months. A jay screeches as I come down to the steps above the house, and a sudden gust of north wind tosses the heads of the trees down in the valley. Grey one minute, fresh and green in their under-leaves the next. I am back at Rovinia, by an open kitchen door.

Autumn Food

Fakes are lentils and *gigantes* butter beans, featured here as Maria's mother cooked them in Liapades Village.

Fakes

This dish can be reheated again and again.

Boil three litres of water in a large saucepan and add half a kilo of lentils. This soup can be reheated indefinitely. Cook for half an hour together with five whole peeled cloves garlic and then add one tin of chopped tomatoes, half a wineglass of olive oil, and salt and pepper to season. Cook further until they have softened. The dish is ready when the liquid is reduced to a thick sauce. Serve the beans with plenty of crusty bread.

Gigantes

Soak 2 lb / 1 kg beans in plenty of tepid water overnight. Then, boil the beans for 30 minutes in the same water until soft. Drain and add fresh cold water. Add to the beans one chopped onion, two small chopped carrots, two sticks of chopped celery, salt and pepper, one wineglass of olive oil, one tin of chopped tomatoes and one tablespoon tomato purée. Then put pan on lowest heat, cover and leave for half an hour.

Chanterelle Mushroom Risotto

Serves 4

1 lb / 500 g chanterelles
1 wineglass olive oil
½ chicken stock cube
1 mug risotto rice
pepper to season

Wash the mushrooms thoroughly: if picked yourself, wash them three or four times to remove the mud. Cut into strips length-wise. Heat the oil in a frying pan until very hot and add the mushrooms. Fry them for 10 minutes then lower the heat and simmer until all their mushroomy liquid evaporates and only the oil remains. Now add the stock cube, season with pepper and cook until all the liquid has gone.

Meanwhile, in a saucepan, heat 2½ mugs of water and when boiling, lower the heat and add the rice. Cover the saucepan and leave on low heat, without stirring, until the water is evaporated.

Add the rice to the chanterelles in the frying pan and stir to mix. Serve piping hot.

Chanterelle Mushroom Soup

Serves 4

Wash and roughly chop 1 lb / 500 g chanterelles to about 1½ cm sizes. Add to a saucepan with three tablespoons of olive oil, half a chicken stock cube and pepper seasoning. Stir over high heat for 10 minutes. Add 1 pint / ½ litre of water, and boil for a further 15 minutes. Stir in two tablespoons of milk and serve immediately with bread.

Chicken Soup

Serves 4

½ chicken
1 whole carrot, lightly scored
1 large onion, lightly scored
1 large potato, skinned and lightly scored
9 oz / 250 g arborio rice
2 eggs
juice of 1 large lemon

Put the chicken and vegetables into a saucepan with 6 pints / 3 litres water. Bring to the boil and simmer for half an hour. After this time, remove the chicken and vegetables. Remove the chicken's skin and take out the bones. Cut the meat into small pieces and return this to the pan with the meat juices.

Add more water to make up to the original level and add the rice. Boil until the rice is tender, though still with a slight 'bite'.

Meanwhile, break the eggs into a bowl, add the lemon juice and beat together. When the soup is ready, take one ladle of soup from pan and add slowly spoonful by spoonful to the eggs and lemon mixture. Beat together for one minute, then pour back into the soup pan and heat through, stirring gently.

Iovarelakia (Little Parcels of Beef)

Serves 4–6

1 lb / 500 g minced beef
1 lb / 500 g arborio rice
1 large onion, chopped
1 wineglass fresh parsley, chopped
3 tablespoons olive oil

2 eggs
juice of 1 lemon
salt and pepper to season

Place all the dry ingredients into a bowl and knead with your hands for five minutes.

In a large saucepan, heat 8 pints / 4 litres of water with some salt, a little pepper and the olive oil. When the water boils, roll up large lumps of the mixture between your hands, like sausages, and lower them into the pan, boiling until the rice is cooked. Set aside in a dish to keep warm while you make the sauce.

Next, break the eggs into a bowl and slowly add the lemon juice — slowly, so as not to curdle the eggs — beating all the while until creamy. Then add a little of the liquid from the pan in which the meat was cooked, beating it in gradually until a smooth consistency is achieved.

Now transfer to a saucepan and stir gently over a low heat for five minutes. Serve poured over the parcels of meat.

Mila Sto Forno (Baked Apples)

Serves 4

4 apples of whatever types you can find — the larger the better
slices of orange
chunky marmalade
4 heaped tablespoons of caster sugar
juice of 2 large oranges

Core the apples, stopping just before you reach the base. Score the skin horizontally round the apples' middles to allow for swelling in cooking. Place them in a baking dish, each upon a slice of orange. Fill the apples' core cavities with marmalade. Sprinkle over the sugar and pour over half of the orange juice, reserving the rest of the juice for later.

Bake the apples in a hot oven for 30 minutes, checking them occasionally and ladling the juices in the dish over the apples as they cook. *Add the remainder of the orange juice 10 minutes before the apples are done.*

Serve hot with Greek yoghurt or cream.

Pomegranate

Like the bat and the narcissus, the pomegranate is associated with the Queen of the Underworld, Persephone, and the arrival of this sweet, pinky-red fruit in autumn makes a good introduction to the months of winter which lie ahead.

Chapter Eleven

Winter

It's cold – but not so cold that the tiny dark irises haven't come up on the slopes of the wild garden. Self-seeded wild narcissi are growing in a clump by the last crumbling steps to the grove. The sea is the same colour as the flowers on the bushy rosemary (they're as tall as trees, some of them, and I used to pull myself by their strong trunks up the steps); a misty grey-blue that looks like an eye bathed in a dilution of indigo and water. But then, when it does grow really cold at Rovinia, I think of the description by Hesiod of the north wind, and I shiver at his account of winter in Greece.

Hesiod on Winter, 700 BC, from *The Penguin Book of Greek Verse* ed. Constantine A. Trypanis, 1971

Avoid the month of Lenaeon – ugly days, all suitable for ox-skinning – and [avoid] the frosts which are cruel, when Boreas [the North Wind] blows over the earth. He blows across horse-breeding Thrace, and stirs up the wide sea; the earth and the forests roar. He falls on many lofty-branched oaks and thick pines and brings them down to the bounteous earth in the mountain glens; and all the vast woods roar, and the beasts shudder and put their tails beneath their genitals, even those whose hide is shaded with fur; for his cold blast blows even through them, though they are shaggy-breasted. He [Boreas] goes through even the ox's hide; it does not hold him back. He also blows through the long-haired goat's skin. But through the sheep's fleeces, because their wool is thick, Boreas' strength does not pierce at all; but he makes the old man run quickly. Yet he does not blow through the soft-skinned girl, who stays at home with her mother, ignorant as yet of the ways of Aphrodite rich in gold; she washes her soft skin carefully and she anoints herself richly with oil, and will lie down in an inner part of the house on a winter's day when the boneless one [the octopus] gnaws his own foot in his fireless house, his miserable abode; for the sun shows him no ground to move to, but circles round the land and the homes of swarthy men, and [only] later shines upon all the Hellenes. Then the creatures of the wood, horned and unhorned, dismally grinding their teeth, flee through the brushwood of the glens, and all have one desire: in their search for shelter to reach some well-protected hiding-place, some rocky cave. Then, like the three-legged man [the old man] whose back is broken and whose head looks down to the ground, they wander to escape the white snow.

And in that season put on, as I tell you, a soft cloak and a fringed tunic to protect your body; and weave a lot of wool on thin warp. Wind this well round you, so that your hair keeps still and does not bristle and stand up all over your body. Lace round your feet well-fitting boots made of the hide of a slaughtered ox, covered thickly inside with felt. And when the season of the frost comes, stitch together skins of firstling kids with ox-sinew to put over your back to keep off the rain. On top, on your head, wear a close-fitting cap of felt to keep your ears dry; for the dawn is cold at the onset of Boreas, and far from the starry sky a mist that will produce good wheat-crops is stretched out across the earth, over the farmlands of blessed men; this is drawn from the ever-flowing rivers, and is lifted high above the earth by wind-storms; and sometimes it turns to rain towards evening, and sometimes to wind, when Thracian Boreas shakes the thick clouds.

It's November 12th, and bright skies, strong sun and a brisk '*Bora Maestro*' – the very wind, surely, which Hesiod warns us against so rigorously – is turning the sea advertisement-blue and the small waves that puff up against the far cliffs are like cigarette smoke expelled from the huge lungs of the Ionian. A tiny iris, half-hidden in the long, rain-fed grass, pokes up on the steps to the back door from the grove and sunken garden, bringing the 'all-the-year-round' spring we have grown quite blasé about in our years on the island. Lemons are green still but growing daily, and bump against our foreheads when we sit on the curved stone seat at the far end of the symmetrical garden my mother made back in the 1960s, with all-white flowers, syringa and canna lilies, and now a forest of wild delphinium taken from one cutting at the monastery above Paleocastritsa. We feel, with a ridiculous optimism, that the worst of Hesiod's winter is over: oranges beam down at us from the tree near Maria and Thodoros' cottage; and, as if determined to provide a new summer out of a hat, the tall arbutus that grows on the slope there is red with its delectable fruit. 'The strawberry tree,' my mother says as we jot down some of Maria's last-night recipes and add some thoughts of our own, 'they look like strawberries and are wonderful with whipped cream. But they taste completely different – and they're a wonderful surprise, appearing in November and going on until the New Year.'

We leave the garden fairly soon – summer fruit and spring flowers or no, the angle of the sun is too low at the tail-end of the year to penetrate this sanctum; and the stone seat, despite our spread macs, is palpably damp. We'll go up the back terrace to the house, pausing to admire the iris; and seeing the last of the cyclamens and bright yellow sternbergia, like outsize crocuses. The best arrival (since Tim and I have had to be back in London for a month and have only just now returned) is a proliferation of white crocuses – the real thing – growing wild as daisies all over the grove that runs directly under the house. Oleander bushes, self-seeded and magnificently tall, look down in their dark leaves at the Christmassy sight of these small, delicate white flowers, each with its small candle of deep yellow inside. Birds, with a distinctly spring-tuned note, are singing loudly in the undisturbed (and, luckily, now protected by law) virgin Mediterranean wood that descends steeply to the olive grove leading to the sea. Tim proclaims that he will go for a swim; and is proved right, if initially thought to be out of his mind to try this halfway through November. The temperature, he announces on returning to the terrace brandishing the thermometer, is 69 °F. The sea is still warm from the long summer months – and we decide not to remind him that it takes just as long to warm up again after winter. Bathing really isn't much of a pleasure until May.

Because the sun is so low in the sky, evening comes sooner than expected after a bright, sunny day. It seems ages ago, in this new paradise of light, that we sat with Maria and heard her ghost stories, mixed in with the village remedies of her youth – cures for indigestion and earache and means of banishing the Evil Eye. But it was certainly part of autumn, and not long past six: the olive-wood fire was lit, and an inky night pressed against the windowpanes, leading us to pull the white cotton curtains across the expanse of unfriendly blackness. Was it only then that we heard from Maria of the woman who had gone to live in a house in Liapades when she was young and had seen each night an other-worldly figure on the stairs, ladling oil from a cup into a dish and back again? This woman had been murdered, so it was said, and a complicated family feud was spelt out for us, with mothers-in-law and nieces and daughters tangled in a web of hatred and reprisal. The ghost is there still, we had been assured; but in this day of innocent blue above an enticing sea sucking at the beach below, it's hard to believe we were actually quite scared that evening by Maria's story. It's been cleared away by the new day, this dark chapter in village history – but then, time here does appear to be immeasurable, guilty only of disappearing too fast into the next to-be-forgotten episode.

Winter is evident, however, even on a sunny day in Corfu Town. Even St Spiridon, one could say, hibernates in his splendid glass coffin: there are almost no tourists here to wake him, and waiters at Aegli and the Corfu Bar are drowsy as end-of-season wasps when we sit at one of the many empty tables. A jeweller's shop, where I spot a tray of minute bead bracelets which might be perfect for my daughter's baby, it is impossible to enter due to the presence of two dogs – each the size of Cerberus – which lie inert on the floor and then jump up to rush out into the crowded street and fight angrily, endangering the legs of would-be shoppers. The market in the street where our lawyer has his office appears to be devoted exclusively to unnameable and strange-looking fish. This is fare for local residents: foreigners would never go for the spiky and scaly creatures on their slabs. And postcards, on the multifarious stands in Capadistriou, the main street that runs parallel to the Liston, hang limp in the November sunlight. With a lengthy trip (from London at least) via Athens to the island, entailing a long wait in Athens airport, few will arrive over the next six months to sample the delights of Corfu. You can almost hear the bustling town kick off its shoes and breathe out in relief at being left alone.

For us, there is a dream of early spring – but the house, even though this is improbable, may be sold by then. Our lawyer, a charming and urbane Corfiot with impeccable connections, tells us from behind an impressive desk in his office, of properties on the market in Corfu: the house by the sea which was claimed by the bank to pay off a debt; the sixty-odd *stremata* in the north of the island where (yet another) British couple have bought and have an urge to build the perfect house. And I'm taken back to the time, forty years ago, when I sat with my parents in the office of the town's estate agent and heard him warn them about the woman from the village 'covered in gold', who wouldn't sell her piece of land until a substantial price was offered. It all seems, as people always say, like yesterday – but here on the island where the blue grows deeper and more intense the further you are from Calabria, it does seem hard to believe it was so long ago. My mother has lived in Corfu for thirty-five years. It's difficult to accept – and fortunately there's no sign of this happening for some time, as viewers for the house are about as thin on the ground as tourists – that one day there will be no house to come to in Corfu.

We drive back to Rovinia and find that winter has perfected our visit with the sight, obtained by Tim as he climbed along the terraces on the far side of the riverbed, of an entire bank of snowdrops. Taller than the English variety; wild, never noticed by us before, the winter flowers, looking down the grove to a deserted beach where a still-warm sea lies waiting for the next storms, are a magnificent sight.

February 2003; snow lies thick on cars outside our London flat and Rovinia has never seemed further away. Maria and

Thodoros ring and say all heat and light are off in the house (why? we can't discover), and they've gone up to the village. It must be cold there too, I conclude – or they wouldn't leave the vaulted sitting room where they often sleep when my mother is away – and I smile when I think of them cooking chops on the olive-wood fire and the ancient, sacrificial smell of burning meat rising to greet potential buyers of the place as they come down the steps.

What will Rovinia be like a year from now? It's as hard to tell as to predict the state of the world we live in. I look in Lawrence Durrell's *Prospero's Cell* and see he reports from Alexandria the terrible bombing of Corfu Town when Germans and Italians fought for possession in 1944, and the miraculous survival of St Spiridon's Church. Could Durrell have foreseen the future of the island, then?

One thing is certain: unless the climate changes beyond recognition, the flowers at Rovinia will mark, as they always have done, the glory of a spring rebirth: the tiny iris that mostly comes in February, the crocus, mallow, pimpernel and poppy – and not forgetting the Judas tree in the riverbed, where the torrent came down three times last month after a record rainfall. However harsh the winter may be at Rovinia, the annual show of spring proper is already underway.

Winter Food

Brisola (Greek Pork Chops)

Beat the chops flat to tenderise the meat, then sprinkle with chopped oregano (*rigani*), brush with olive oil and season with salt and pepper. Grill – ideally over a barbecue – and eat the chops with *salamura* sauce. Boiled rice or fried potatoes go equally well with this dish.

Maria's vegetable broth. This is made as a purée to which one adds as much water to taste to make it up into the soup. It can be thick and chunky as an evening meal or thin as a first course. The purée will keep in the fridge for up to five days after it is made.

Suppa Maria

Serves 6

6 medium-sized carrots, peeled and chopped
5 onions, chopped
4 large potatoes, peeled and chopped into small pieces
2 large sticks of celery, chopped
large bunch parsley, chopped
½ wineglass olive oil
salt and pepper to season

In a saucepan, combine all the ingredients and season. Add water to cover and stir. Lid the pan and boil for 30 minutes or until the water has evaporated and the vegetables are very soft.

Liquidise in a blender and store in the fridge in a jam-jar or airtight container.

Psarosuppa (Fish Soup)

Serves 6–8

2 lbs / 1 kg good white fish
8 pints / 4 litres water
3 tablespoons olive oil
1 large onion, peeled and quartered
3 carrots, peeled and chopped
1 lb / 500 g celery, cut into 4 inch strips
1 lb / 500 g potatoes, peeled and chopped into pieces
salt and pepper to season

Clean and wash the fish. Place in a saucepan with the water, oil and seasoning. You may need to cut the fish in two, crossways, to fit the pan. Boil fast for 10 minutes. Remove the fish and set aside for use in another recipe.

Now, to the fish stock add the onion, carrots, potatoes and celery. Boil until tender. Serve in bowls, squeezing in lemon juice as you eat it, and a little black pepper.

Although they used only to be available in spring and summer in Corfu, leeks are now always in season.

Leek Moussaka

Serves 6

3 lbs / 1½ kg leeks, washed and chopped into 2 inch rounds
2 lbs / 1 kg minced lamb
1 onion, chopped
1 wineglass fresh basil, chopped
1 bay leaf
½ wineglass olive oil
1 heaped tablespoonful tomato purée
salt, and black and red pepper to season

béchamel sauce
graviera cheese, grated

Heat a little olive oil in a casserole dish and fry the onion. Add red and black pepper, salt, the bay leaf and basil and cook, stirring continuously, for 10 minutes. Add the mince and cook for a couple of minutes, then add the tomato purée. Still stirring, cook for a further 10 minutes. In another pan, gently sweat the leeks in the half wineglass of olive oil and cook for 20 minutes.

In an ovenproof dish, layer the leeks, then the mince mixture and season with a little salt. Cook in a medium–low oven for 20 minutes.

Meanwhile, make a béchamel sauce, adding an egg for lightness. Remove the dish from the oven and spread this sauce over its top. Grate a little graviera cheese on top and return to the oven until the cheese melts and begins to brown.

Caramelised Oranges

Serves 6

3 large Washington navel oranges
7 oz / 200 g granulated sugar
7 oz / 200 g almonds
whipped cream

Peel all the skin and pith from the oranges and slice them in half across their middles. Place in a dish and sprinkle over a little sugar.

Heat the rest of the sugar in a small saucepan, allowing it to brown, without stirring it or adding water. Remove the pan from the heat, add two tablespoons of boiling water – standing well back as it will spit – and stir. If the sugar sticks to the pan, return to the heat until it softens. Pour the sugar mixture into a buttered shallow baking tin. Meanwhile, skin the almonds, fry in a little oil until light brown and set aside to cool. Once the sugar mixture is set cold, bend its tin slightly to loosen the caramel. Transfer the caramel to a dishcloth and break it up by beating with a hammer or pestle.

Sprinkle the caramel pieces over the oranges. Cover the oranges with whipped cream and decorate with the almonds.

Arbutus Unedo

Arbutus unedo is the Latin name of the *koumara*, the Greek strawberry tree which grows wild and abundant in Corfu. From November to January the fruit is ripe and is delectable eaten with whipped cream and sugar.

The Village

Maria's Remedies

Stomachache
Corfu is famous for its range of wild greens, or *horta*. This lovely sounding selection of weeds makes a broth used to calm stomachache or indigestion. No amounts or exact translations are given here: these are Corfiot wild greens and can be found growing in the spring, in meadows and on cliffs. Where well known, their English names appear.

Horta

zegounous

zakoulies

prekalida (dandelion leaves)

sinapia

malathra (fennel)

moscolathana (a weed with a lovely smell)

kokinogouli (a wild beet, sister of the cultivated beet, sescla)

Boil the ingredients together until al dente to make a medicinal soup. Add oil or a squeeze of lemon as required.

Horta can also be served in their own right with cheese – *graviera*, Gouda or white *mezithra* (a soft cheese) – and makes a wonderful lunch or supper.

Headache

Maria has successfully treated a good number of headache-bound visitors with this compress.

Soak a napkin in a mixture of half iced water, half wine vinegar and apply to the forehead. Refresh and reapply the napkin every five minutes for half an hour.

Chest cold, with difficulty in breathing

Maria's inhalation for chest congestion. There is a great quantity of wild sage at Rovinia, and this infusion is efficacious.

Put 2 pints / 1 litre of water in a saucepan with three branches of sage. Boil fast for 10 minutes. Pour into bowl and, bending over it, place towel over the head.

Earache

Dip a swab of cotton wool in hot olive oil and place in the affected ear.

Cuts

Maria swears by this …

Wash the cut thoroughly with urine or cigarette ash.

Scorpion bite
Soak a cloth with ammonia and apply to the affected area immediately.

Diarrhoea
Cut two to three wild blackberry branches, boil in water for 30 minutes and drink by the mugful. Alternatively, eat a tablespoonful of strong Turkish coffee.

Indigestion (or hangovers)
A basil or rosemary tea. These are plentiful herbs in Corfu, and 'mountain tea', famous in Greece for curing hangovers, is made from boiling and straining the scented herbs of the hills.

Insomnia
Drink a rosemary tea before bedtime as above.

Piles
Boil together one large mug each of vinegar and water. Pour this into a bowl and sit on it. None of us could find the courage to try this one.

Maria & Thodoros' Chronology of Olives

Olives, 'a taste older than meat,' in the words of Lawrence Durell, 'older than wine. A taste as old as cold water.'

Olive oil, the 'liquid gold' of Homer and 'great therapeutic' of Hippocrates, has been the pride and joy of Corfu ever since the Venetians decided to make the island so rich in trees that the city in the sea would never go short of it. The dark, almost greenish colour of oil on the island removes it from Tuscan or Provençal examples; and to me, at least, it is infinitely more delicious. A hunk of bread and a Greek tomato the size of a baby's head need only a saucer of the magic stuff to provide a wonderful meal. If olives, very small at Rovinia but with a bitter, woody taste that is quite unmistakable, are added to this feast, then, as we say laughing, we're really sampling the Greek experience.

Oil for Aladdin's lamp: the first artificial light, as early as the Olympiad of 776 BC, derived from olive oil, and the knowledge passed from the Phoenicians to the Greeks. Athena, the goddess of wisdom, planted an olive tree at the gates of the Acropolis, and the gods of Greece were said to have been born under the branches of the olive tree. It's impossible to imagine the island without its tapestry of olives, some so vast and ancient they seem more like mythical monsters from under a sea once covering all the Ionian Kingdom than trees. In winter, bundles of olives stand by the side of untravelled roads, waiting to be taken to the mill. No one goes without their own crop and oil, and Maria and Thodoros are proprietors of the olive orchard at Rovinia. It's theirs to crush, marinate in brine, or take in sacks up to Liapades. And their generosity shows when the jam-jar of olives on the hall table marks the departure of a favoured guest or family member. For days after a reluctant return to the city, the scent of Rovinia olives (and the oil, taken with care, to make it last) fill the flat. Memories of nets spread under trees and the small fruit as green as apples and then darkening as winter draws in, come to haunt us.

Olives – the oil

'In November and December we put small trees – *mouri* – in the ground, five metres apart, dig a hole and pour in water until they're standing in mud. We cover them well with earth and pat down firmly. They need rainwater in summer in their first year. We dig around the base of the trees to weed, add 1 kilo of fertiliser each November and prune them, and in ten years they bear real fruit.

'In five years we have small fruit, and cut the grass below each tree. We spread nets, and five times in winter we collect the crop. We shake out the rotten ones from the collecting sieve and put the good ones in big sacks to take to the mill. There's a great barrel, and we throw in our olives; the machine turns them in water and then they go up into a greater barrel where they're smashed and crushed. All the *mourga* – rubbish – comes out and channels divide the rubbish water from the good oil. Seven big sackfuls of olives makes 10 gallons of oil.'

Olives – to eat

'In five years from planting the trees, in January and later, we take the good small olives – they must be black – and place them for a whole month in a barrel with water. We don't empty the barrel, but leave them in the water and keep filling the barrel up. After the month is up, we lower the olives into a big bucket and wash them with our hands, stirring them round and round. We throw water on the olives and let it run over them. We wash them like this many times, hosing them down.

'Then, we wash the barrel and in a bowl, we put 1 kilo of salt, some handfuls of chopped *rigani* and, each cut into quarters, eight lemons. We put the olives back into their barrel and place them in layers with the salt, the lemons and the herbs. Twenty days they must be left, with water.

'Then, we put another kilo of salt in a pail, and half-fill that pail with more water. We melt the salt into the water with our hands and float in an egg – when the egg begins to sink, we know to add more salt: another half kilo. The egg must show just its tip above the water, then we remove it and pour this water on top of all the olives. It must cover the olives and must be left for another month.

'After this next month, we taste the olives and if they're still bitter, we leave them longer in the salty water as it takes away their bitterness.

'Two months is the most time it should take to prepare olives good to eat.'

Herbs at Rovinia

It is impossible to imagine Rovinia – or indeed Greek cooking at all – without the herbs which grow so abundantly on the hills, and even a thousand cups of the soothing *tsai tou vounou* (mountain tea) uses up an invisible amount of them.

Fennel was considered by the Greeks and Hindus to be a potent sexual stimulant, and in the Dionysiac festivities crowns of fennel leaves were worn and the seeds used as aphrodisiacs.

Thyme, without which the lamb cooked for Sunday lunch would seem dull and tasteless, was in use from early times in massage and bath oils. Those scented by thyme were regarded as elegant.

The lovely sounding *rigani* – the Greek version of Italian oregano – is the most used herb in Greece. Also very similar to marjoram, it grows wild and was known as 'the joy of the mountain'.

Fennel

Go down the west coast, land on a deserted beach and find wild fennel, or *marathra* as Maria terms it, and make a tea that aids digestion and calms the nerves. It grows in the bay at Iliodorus alongside samphire and is delicious eaten as a salad after simmering in boiling water for a few seconds.

Borage

Borage grows early in the year along the donkey-paths and at the sides of country lanes, bright blue with thistly leaves. This most summer-Pimms-at-the-Vicarage of herb wild flowers is the base for the first strong narcotic potion recorded: Homer's Nepenthe which brings instant and total forgetfulness. Pliny and Discorides give this recipe, of borage steeped in red wine. But it's impossible not to feel that the recipe must have included a poisonous ingredient – probably the scarlet and white deadly fungus, *ammonita muscaria*.

Rosemary

The most faithful and sturdy of herbs, aiding memory and making a blue garden at Rovinia all the way down to the sea. With lamb and with *barbounia* (red mullet), storm-resistant and caring nothing for the salt-laden west wind or the freezing *Maestro*, this evergreen blooms and smells sweet all year round.

Sage

Sage likes to march down the steps and gravel paths at Rovinia that go down to the sea, its leaves like rabbits' ears and pale flowers as stubborn in stormy weather as the rosemary's.

Thyme

With a woody, sturdy nature, wild thyme makes up the natural kitchen range of herbs that have embraced the hillside since Rovinia was built, covering scars in the stone and forming an uninterrupted Mediterranean forest to match the hill opposite. Thyme, rosemary and sage are the mainstays here; for an infusion, for a meal cooked outdoors – or for a banquet.

Laurel

In Greek myth, Daphne was a huntress and had no need for suitors – when the god Apollo pursued her, she prayed to the river-god for deliverance and was changed into a laurel tree.

Basil

Not used for cooking in Greece as it was said to grow at the entrance to the Underworld in order to remind people of the beauty of the world they left behind, though the Greeks are happy to sprinkle the tiny leaves on tomatoes and add rich, deep golden olive oil to make a perfect salad.

Local Drinks & Wines

Ouzo, which mysteriously only tastes good in Greece, comes with a glass of water on the side, and the water, from a wellspring, is what makes this drink so wonderful.

Tsipourro, originally from Crete and the equivalent of a French marc, is a colourless and wildly intoxicating distillation made at the end of the grape harvest from must-residue. It should be dashed down after an early swim in the sea.

'*Kourtaki*' *retsina* I think especially good when sitting on the terrace of the Nikterida, though we also order the excellent local wines of Liapades.

Liapaditiko is a good wine made by the Goulis family, which includes the cardiologist Dr Goulis who cared for my father when he became ill at Rovinia. All the Goulis family comes from Liapades.

Agirou, also from the Liapades area and considered very good, comes from a white grape which has a little of the strawberry grape in its bouquet.

Moschato is a light white wine from Pantocrator, and a good aperitif.

Saints

Saints Jason and Sosipatros first taught Christianity on the island in the first century, and a beautiful small Byzantine church, St Jason and Sosipatros, stands on the western fringes of Corfu Town, complete with neat flower-beds bursting with marigolds and roses and a strolling *pappas* or two. But it was the arrival of St Spiridon, brought from Cyprus a millennium or so after his death, who supplied miracles and protection against raids and conquests.

St Spiridon was born in Cyprus in 270 AD and was a poor shepherd who worked miracles all his life. When the Saracens took over Cyprus his grave was opened in order to remove his sanctified remains to Constantinople, and his body was found to be intact, while a scent of basil, a sign of saintliness, came from the grave. At the fall of Constantinople in 1453, he was brought to Corfu and passed into the possession of the Voulgaris family (Marily, whose *mezes* are described in this book, is a descendant) before being transferred to the present church bearing his name in town. St Spiridon's companion on this journey was St Theodora, a Byzantine empress famous for restoration of icon worship in Byzantium. Theodora can be found in the Orthodox Metropolitan Church in the town; she works miracles to this day.

Saints Spiridon and Theodora are the focus for litanies and services several times a year with Spiridon brought from his silver and ebony sarcophagus on important days for the island.

A Brief Calendar of Festivals & Holidays

January 6th

Epiphany. More celebrated than Christmas, this religious festival includes the blessing of holy waters in the harbour of Mandraki under Corfu Town's old fortress.

March 8th

Saint's Day for St Theodora. Her effigy in the shape of a doll carries a watermelon on her head, which is then handed out to the crowd.

Clean Monday

The first day of Lent. Olives and taramasalata are eaten at country picnics.

Carnival

This takes place on the Sunday one week before Lent and again on the following Sunday, just before Lent. The Carnival is one of the most famous in Greece – for its dancing, music and street theatre. Together, Carnival and Easter make as much of a mark on island life as they did in Venetian times.

Palm Sunday

Services are also performed for the anniversary of Corfu's salvation by St Spiridon from the plague in 1629.

Easter Sunday

Greek Easter is of course well known and, along with Carnival, is the biggest holiday in Corfu's calendar. The nearest village to Rovinia to celebrate with lavish festivities is Lakones, above Paleocastritsa, and often covered by the black clouds of rain and thunder. The monastery at Paleocastritsa itself celebrates its Feast Day on the first Friday following the holiday, and hundreds of people attend.

Easter in Corfu Town begins on the morning of Easter Saturday with the first Resurrection Ceremony after carrying the litanies of St Spiridon. The ceremony is accompanied by the sound of crashing ceramic pots as they are tossed from windows and balconies, which marks the throwing out of Judas Iscariot, betrayer of Jesus, who was a Corfiot. In the evening, a Resurrection Ceremony takes place in the Upper Square of the town; the priests chant Easter hymns and candles shine in the houses of the square.

August 11th

For a long time in 1716 the Turks besieged the island and Corfiot forces were much depleted. St Spiridon appeared at a critical moment, holding a candle and a cross.

August 15th

The Day of the Blessed Virgin. One of the largest of the many festivals on the island takes place at Kassiopi – now known, as a result of the second British invasion, as Kensington-on-Sea.

October 28th, Oxi Day

Oxi Day (No Day) marks the day when Greece said a resounding 'No' to Mussolini.

First Sunday in November

Services are carried out to mark St Spiridon's saving of the island from a deadly cholera epidemic in 1673.

Walks for the Visitor
by Tim Owens

Gardelades

Across from Liapades, set on top of a craggy spine of land less than half a kilometre away, is the small village of Gardelades. Little of importance happens here these days, although up until fairly recently, it was one of the local centres for olive-pressing. If you walk up from the steep, twisting road that leads into the village, you will find on the roadside, just at the edge of the village entrance, a well-preserved and painted steel olive-pressing machine – a totemic reminder of its past role in the business. When that business closed down recently, the rest of the village reverted to its old sleepy ways.

Because it is situated just off the main tourist beats, Gardelades has remained as simple an old-style Corfiot village as you will find in this neighbourhood, and it is worth visiting for that reason alone. There are no tavernas and modern shops, and although the tiny main square has been remodelled and relaid in new stone with the help of local government grants, the rest of the village is as old as it ever was. The main feature of the village is the surprising cluster of three separate churches, around which the rest of the village houses seem to cling. With its tiny local population and minimal car traffic coming and going into the place, and with its time-warped sleepy atmosphere, it makes for a very pleasant and quiet walk on a warm bright day. It gives one a very convincing feeling of what village life must have been like before the advent of tourism and the modernisation that came with it.

The main surrounding views on offer are over to the east of the Plain of Ropa, and the neighbouring village of Liapades, just opposite to the south. And from the very western end of the village, one can see the area of the Bay of Liapades, and the more famous village of Paleocastritsa beyond.

Doukades and Surrounds

Leaving Gardelades down a winding road on the north side of this small, craggy hillside and through a beautiful swathe of dark and ancient olive groves, the route leads out of the village, down and across the 'old' Paleocastritsa–Corfu Town road, and then up hill again towards the next neighbouring village of Doukades, a further half-kilometre away. This slightly larger and more modern village is tucked under the imposing rock face of the stubby Arakli mountain range. Although just as 'off the beaten track' from the tourist point of view as Gardelades, this village nevertheless has a bit more of a bustle about it; a fact mainly explained by that the main road running through it leads to the more important village of Skripero, three kilometres beyond. (The much larger village of Skripero is still to this day the civic administrative headquarters of the north-west region and contains the main police station the main post office, and the mayoral offices that control and look after all the surrounding villages.)

In the main square of Doukades, you will find two or three modern mini-market type shops, a well-spoken-of local butcher's shop, and a couple of small restaurant-cum-bar establishments that front on to the square – all of which cater for the local community throughout the year, regardless of low or high season influences. It is for both tourists and local people alike a very pleasant place to break one's journey with a meal, a drink or a snack.

Parts of the old village and the main local church still exist, but it is noticeable that a lot more modern architecture is on view in and around the fringes of the village. A huge recent addition to the village landscape is an imposing new structure built by the Theotoki family – a famous and distinguished old Corfiot family – to house, allegedly, their library and other personal papers. Set in private grounds and behind a high wall, it is the dominating building of the village.

There is little to see in the rest of the main huddle of the village other than to admire the creative gardening efforts of the locals. Here, depending on the season, one can see an array of closely pruned orange trees, fig trees, and hanging bunches of bougainvillaea and morning glory, as well as all the other flowers found on the island. The neatness of their individual efforts and the evident care with which they go about their gardening habits is something you come to notice in all of the surrounding villages, even in the smallest and most out of the way of them.

But it is on the road behind the westerly side of the village and hugging the overhanging rock face of the Arakli mountain shelf that one gets the best vantage point of the village and its location. Here, along a winding road (recently tarmaced and wide enough for cars), the route climbs upwards alongside the rock face, offering the traveller a view back over the village below and across the Plain of Ropa as it spreads eastwards and southwards to the other side of the island. The further up the road one goes, the more one can see, and on a clear day one can see not only Corfu Town, with the Bay of Garitsa behind it, but even the length of the Corfu Channel and the range of mountains of the Epirus on the mainland beyond. If the light is right, the whole vista can be seen in the most extraordinary and sharp focus. It is particularly impressive in the late afternoon, when the sinking sun in the west casts its final glow across towards the east of the island. Every village in between along the Plain of Ropa appears to be in full view as it is picked out by the sunlight.

At some point along this climbing road, and on the left hand side, there is a sign indicating a footpath that leads up to the vertiginously located chapel of St Simeon, perched high up on one of the topmost ledges of Mount Arakli. The walk up to this chapel takes the best part of forty-five minutes. But if you make it you will be rewarded with an even more spectacular view, this time taking in the whole panoramic sweep of this north-western part of the island.

To the east is the view of the Plain of Ropa, with Corfu Town beyond; to the south is the spine of the mountain range that leads from the Ermones region and down to the southern tip of the island; and to the west there is the whole sweep of Rovinia Bay and the rest of the coastline leading to Paleocastritsa itself, with its famous monastery of Our Lady of the Virgin Mary (the original site of which goes back to the thirteenth century), and all the land around which is generally associated with the name of Paleocastritsa, even though that name really only truly belongs to the small bay beneath the local monastery.

Back down again in the main square of Doukades, an alternative walk is to follow the road going northwards out of the village towards Skripero, roughly three kilometres away. About halfway along this beautiful winding country road, one can turn off into some narrower lanes that lead into some of the most idyllic scenery to be found in this part of the island. Here, the peace and quiet in the surrounding fields and cultivated land all around is a wonderful experience for the keen walker. At the right time of the year in spring or autumn the wild flowers on view seem to stretch forever into the distance. And in the silence all around you can hear the most extraordinary symphony of song provided by the local birdlife. It is possible to see or hear everything from the nightingales, linnets, goldfinches and woodchats to shrikes and Sardinian warblers. The feeling of remoteness is so overwhelming that, if and when a car passes by, it comes of something as a surprise and shock to realise that one is near to human habitation at all, so great is the feeling of isolation. And yet one is never more than a couple of kilometres from the nearest village.

The Plain of Ropa

The main road from Liapades to Corfu Town cuts across the low-lying Plain of Ropa in the middle of the island, and has the narrow Ropa River running through it in a north–south line. Here, this flat, open space of land turns out on a closer inspection to be an almost seamless grid of plots of farmland and private allotments that mostly belong to the communities of the neighbouring villages of Kanakades, Marmaro and Gianades. It is a very open and exposed location, and so it is not recommended as a walk on a hot day due to the lack of shade to be found. However, on milder days the main fun of walks in this area is to follow the numerous irrigation channels that criss-cross the plain while looking out for the frogs and toads that hug the damp reed beds of the nearby streams. Sometimes the noise of their rhythmic croaking calls can be the loudest sounds of the entire neighbourhood.

Odysseus' Rock

If you have reached as far as the Plain of Ropa by car, then the next best drive-cum-walk from this location is to drive two or three kilometres away to the overlooking village of

Gianades, perched on the slopes of the spine of mountainous land that forms the chain heading down to the south of the island. Leave the car parked conveniently near the main village square and take the path that leads south-westwards straight out of the square. Follow this path through a woodland area heading towards the west coast of the island. After about a kilometre or so of shaded walking, it is possible to reach a high vantage point of what is, effectively, the western cliff-face of the north-west part of the island. From here you can look out across the expanse of the Ionian Sea and in the general direction of the toe and heel of Italy. Below in the sea, and a mere kilometre or so from the shoreline, you should be able to see the solitary island rock known locally as Odysseus' Rock – so called because seen from some angles, its shape resembles the silhouette of an upturned shipwreck, its rudder and keel both pointing skywards. And it is this rock, and its local name, which give some credibility to the legend of Odysseus having first been shipwrecked and then washed up on one of the local beaches, possibly even that of Rovinia itself.

Mount Arakli to Lakones

The best view of the whole of the Paleocastritsa and Rovinia Bay environment – whether land, sea or shoreline – is obtained by making the walk from the top of Mount Arakli down to the village of Lakones, perched halfway down the cliff-face. To reach this well-known cliff-top walk, one has first to drive up to the main road on top of Mount Arakli.

To achieve this you drive first towards the village of Skripero and then follow the winding road as it heads up to a hilltop village called Troumpeta, near the top of the climb. From here, take a left turn towards the signposted village of Makrades. At about the halfway point on this road, and five kilometres or so from Makrades, there is a signpost on the left-hand side of the road indicating a local chapel built on top of the cliff edge of Mount Arakli. The walkers should be dropped off at this point while the driver continues on the road into Makrades and then down and on into the village of Lakones to meet the walking party later.

The walkers, meanwhile, having walked the half a kilometre or so to the cliff-top chapel on Mount Arakli, find themselves staring down at the whole coastline around the Paleocastritsa area. It is the most stunning view of the north-western neighbourhood of the island of Corfu. With the extra height (Mount Arakli is over four hundred metres above sea-level) the visitor can look down and see all the local bays and the rest of the coastline as it stretches down towards the south of the island. And taking as a marker the small island rock, Odysseus' Rock, in the sea below, one can quite easily follow the path of Odysseus' floating, shipwrecked body as he would have drifted up to the safety of one of the local bays, with King Alcinous' palace, quite plausibly, being located in what is now the famous monastery at Paleocastritsa. The geography and all the other local legends associated with this part of the island lend themselves perfectly to the Homeric story.

One can play around with the various permutations of this ancient story while looking on and walking down this beautiful cliff-top walk into the village of Lakones. And in between thinking about facts of ancient history and folklore associated with the vicinity, one can admire the slightly more alpine flowers to be found at this higher altitude as well as noticing the occasional presence of darting and swooping swifts, who, with their longer wingspans, distinguish themselves from their more abundant and common cousins, the swallows, that come and go throughout the Mediterranean region.

9416 (174)

www.summersdale.com